Digital Twin Technology

A Simplified Guide for Everyone

NOVA MARTIAN

Disclaimer

This book has been created with the assistance of AI tools for content generation, editing, and formatting. While AI tools have contributed to its development, the content has been reviewed to ensure its quality and accuracy. Readers are encouraged to approach the material critically and verify information where necessary.

Contents

Introduction

In recent years, technological innovation has brought about transformative changes in how businesses operate, how cities are managed, and how individuals interact with the world. Among these technological advancements, digital twin technology has emerged as a groundbreaking concept, promising to revolutionize various industries through the creation of precise, dynamic digital replicas of physical entities. This book, "Digital Twin Technology: A Simplified Guide for Everyone," aims to provide a clear, concise, and accessible exploration of this complex and multifaceted subject, tailored specifically for general readers who may not have a technical background.

At its core, a digital twin is a digital replica of a physical object, process, or system. It operates by using real-time data, analytics, and advanced simulation techniques to mirror the physical counterpart it represents. This mirroring allows for an in-depth understanding of the performance characteristics, operational scenarios, and potential improvements for the physical entity. Digital twins can simulate, predict, and optimize outcomes, offering unprecedented insights and opportunities for innovation and efficiency.

The concept of digital twins has evolved significantly since its inception. Initially conceptualized and employed by NASA to improve the reliability and performance of space systems, digital twins have since expanded their reach into numerous fields such as manufacturing, healthcare, construction, transportation, and energy, among others. They offer tangible benefits, such as reducing maintenance costs, enhancing safety, optimizing performance, and ultimately driving better decision-making processes.

As digital twin technology becomes increasingly prevalent, it is accompanied by challenges that must be carefully navigated. Balancing the benefits with complexities such as data integration, system interoperability, and scalability requires careful consideration and expertise. Moreover, issues surrounding data privacy, security, and ethical use further complicate the implementation of digital twins in various contexts.

This book is structured to provide a comprehensive yet straightforward introduction to digital twin technology. Each chapter delves into critical aspects, from understanding the foundational principles and historical development to exploring practical applications and identifying future trends. Readers will gain a thorough grasp of how digital twins work, their significance in modern technological ecosystems, and the ethical considerations and privacy implications that accompany their use.

In crafting this guide, the aim is to empower readers with the knowledge and understanding needed to appreciate the potential digital twin technology holds and to engage thoughtfully with its applications and implications. As industries continue to embrace digital technologies and the interconnected nature of the Internet of Things grows, digital twin technology stands out as a pivotal element in shaping the future landscape of innovation. This book invites you to explore this fascinating and rapidly evolving field, equipping you with the insights needed to comprehend its impact and envision its possibilities.

2

Chapter 1

Introduction to Digital Twin Technology

Digital twin technology represents a digital replica of a physical object or system, enabling real-time monitoring and analysis. It harnesses data from sensors and advanced analytics to enhance decision-making and optimize performance. Initially developed for aerospace applications, digital twins have expanded into diverse industries, transforming manufacturing, healthcare, and urban planning. This chapter uncovers the fundamental components, historical progression, and common misconceptions surrounding digital twins, offering a foundational understanding of their growing influence in modern technology.

1.1 Understanding Digital Twins

Picture a bustling metropolis. The streets pulse with life; vehicles snake through intersections, buildings stand as stoic witnesses to the ever-thrumming urban dance. Now imagine being able to control, analyze, and predict every aspect of this city's function, from the flow of traffic to the temperature of each building, without ever leaving your desk. Welcome to the world of digital twins.

At its core, a digital twin is a digital replica of a phys-

ical object, system, or process. Created by integrating
data from sensors and other sources, these virtual models provide real-time insights into their physical counterparts. This allows us to monitor operations, diagnose
problems, and even predict outcomes—all without physical intervention. To the uninitiated, this might seem like
the stuff of science fiction, yet it's very much contemporary reality.

Digital twin technology finds its origins in the aerospace
industry, where engineers sought to create reliable simulations of spacecraft and aircraft systems long before a
physical model had been assembled. In this pioneering
setting, digital twins played a pivotal role in reducing
risks and cutting costs associated with the intricacies of
flight. But what, precisely, makes a digital twin shimmer
to life?

A digital twin is composed of three quintessential components: a physical entity, its digital counterpart, and
the connection that facilitates an ongoing exchange of
data between the two. Picture a wind turbine, the physical entity towering in its remote field, feeling the force
of each gust of wind. In a control room miles away, a detailed 3D model—the digital twin—mimics the real-time
status of the turbine blades spinning, its internal mechanisms humming under stress. The data link between
the turbine and its digital twin is constantly streaming,
capturing health information, current operational status,
and environmental conditions.

The utilization of digital twins extends far beyond the
confines of aviation and energy sectors. Think of smart
cities, where digital twins of urban infrastructure provide unparalleled levels of control. Authorities can preemptively tackle congestion by modeling traffic scenarios or curtail energy use by simulating temperature controls in buildings. In healthcare, a digital twin of a hu-

4

man heart could allow doctors to simulate and visualize how different treatments affect individual patients, without trial and error on their bodies.

Unlike static paper models or basic computer simulations, digital twins are dynamic entities. They evolve, reflecting the changes occurring to their physical doubles. This continuous adaptation makes them indispensable for optimizing operations within complex systems. Consider the auto racing industry, where every competitive edge matters: engineers use digital twins to test aerodynamic modifications or predict vehicle performance under a variety of conditions. Similarly, in manufacturing, digital twins enable real-time adjustments to machinery, enhancing output and efficiency.

The beauty of digital twins lies in their predictive power. By analyzing data trends and spotting anomalies, these digital doubles can forecast potential issues before they occur. This proactive feature is particularly beneficial in domains such as power grid management, where preventing a malfunction can save vast amounts of energy and resources, not to mention the inconvenience to consumers. Moreover, sectors driven by precision and timing, like logistics, find a natural ally in digital twins. By simulating supply chain routes and predicting delays, companies can adjust to real-time conditions, saving time and reducing costs.

Yet, as transformative as they are, digital twins present their own set of challenges. The data required to render a digital twin useful must be robust, comprehensive, and, most importantly, accurate. Errors or omissions can lead to flawed models that misrepresent real-world conditions, leading to suboptimal or even harmful decisions. Privacy concerns also arise, especially when personal data is incorporated into digital models, necessitating stringent oversight and robust security measures.

Furthermore, creating a true digital twin can be a resource-intensive endeavor, requiring sophisticated technology and significant investment. But these initial hurdles are balanced by long-term gains. The reduction in downtime, optimized resource use, and enhanced decision-making processes can ultimately lead to significant cost savings and operational efficiencies.

Innovation in digital twin technology continues to push boundaries. With developments in artificial intelligence, the ability of digital twins to learn and adapt independently is becoming attainable. This opens up possibilities for self-optimizing systems that adjust to environmental changes without human intervention. Imagine a digital twin of a residential solar panel system that autonomously alters energy capture settings based on weather forecasts, maximizing efficiency and minimizing waste without homeowner input.

Moreover, as the Internet of Things (IoT) proliferates, the interconnectedness of our digital and physical worlds will become even more intrinsic. Each 'thing' within the IoT network—a sensor, a vehicle, a home appliance—has the potential to be part of a larger digital twin ecosystem, providing a more comprehensive picture of our environments and how we interact with them.

Digital twins are reshaping how we comprehend and engage with the world. They offer a glimpse into the future, where data and reality coexist seamlessly, allowing us to innovate with precision and foresight. As their capabilities expand and their applications become more widespread, digital twins will undoubtedly remain a cornerstone of technological evolution, forming the intricate fabric of a digitally augmented reality.

1.2 Historical Context and Development

The genesis of digital twin technology is neither accidental nor rapid. It has gradually woven itself into the fabric of technological evolution, stemming from a confluence of advancements across various fields. To better appreciate its story, it is imperative to trace the roots through a historical tapestry that begins long before the term "digital twin" was coined.

A fitting starting point is the realm of aviation and aerospace, industries defined by their unforgiving demand for accuracy and innovation. In the 1960s, the race to space conjured the need for reliable ways to simulate and test technologies without risking the gargantuan costs associated with failure. NASA, with its constellation of projects stretching across infinite realms of possibility, ventured into this territory. During the Apollo program, the idea of simulating spacecraft systems through comprehensive models played a critical role. The "physical twin" methodology developed here—an early form of creating precise replicas for testing—paved the way for what would eventually become digital twins.

As the clock advanced into the latter half of the 20th century, the computing revolution sparked a transformation that would lay the foundation for digital innovation. It was the 1980s and 1990s when the seeds of digital twin technology truly began to germinate. The proliferation of powerful computers and the digitization of processes allowed industries to transcend beyond

7

basic physical replicas into more sophisticated virtual models.

Product lifecycle management (PLM) emerged as a vital concept during this period. Originally conceived as a method to manage the lifecycle of a product from inception through engineering, design, and manufacture, it became a precursor to modern digital twins. By collecting and utilizing lifecycle data, companies began to see the benefits of crafting digital representations that could adapt and inform real-world processes. PLM systems were, in a sense, digital progeny—complex in design and dynamic in purpose.

The dawn of the 21st century heralded another leap forward. Data—by now recognized as a new form of currency—became ubiquitous. Advancements in sensor technology and the increased connectivity of devices through the burgeoning Internet of Things (IoT) catalyzed the need for more precise and dynamic digital models. This period saw the formalization of "digital twins" as a distinct concept. As computing power burgeoned, so too did the capacity to simulate complex systems with precision and depth inconceivable in earlier decades.

One illustrative example of digital twin deployment can be found in the automotive sector, where virtual replicas of vehicles allowed manufacturers to test every conceivable parameter under simulated conditions before physical production even began. General Motors, for instance, leveraged digital twins to enhance the design and manufacturing processes, leading to significant cost and time savings. This approach heralded a profound shift in how products could be developed, from conception to implementation, fundamentally transforming industrial practices.

Parallel to this evolution was the increasing sophistication of software algorithms, capable of processing vast amounts of data with unprecedented speed and accuracy. Machine learning, a subset of artificial intelligence that focuses on building systems capable of self-improvement from data, also began to find synergy with digital twin technology, enabling predictive analytics within these models. This development not only enhanced the reliability of digital twins but also expanded their potential applications.

The oil and gas industry became an early adopter as well, grappling with complex systems that required intricate modeling for enhanced efficiency and safety. Digital twins became invaluable in planning and predictive maintenance, reducing downtime through simulations capable of foretelling equipment failures based on historical data analyzed by these intelligent systems.

As we traverse the digital twin timeline, it becomes evident that its development is inextricably linked to the broader technological trends of the era—each advancement a stone on the pathway to sophistication. The convergence of big data, artificial intelligence, and IoT technologies continues to inject energy into the digital twin paradigm, cementing its role in industry after industry.

To understand the future trajectory of digital twins, we must revisit the lessons from their history. The incremental advancements—each a building block— illustrate the profound impact that interdisciplinary collaboration has had. Fields that once navigated separate pathways now find themselves intertwined, with digital twin technology at the nexus, serving as a testament to how innovation can defy boundaries.

As we stride into an increasingly digital future, the prospect of further innovations looms large. The continuing development of edge computing, which enables the processing of data closer to the source of generation, promises to enhance the real-time responsiveness of digital twins, adding new layers of functionality and efficiency. Industries are not merely adopting digital twins; they are crafting ecosystems where digital twins interact, learn, and evolve, suggesting that the most exciting chapters in their story are still unwritten.

Thus, the historical context and development of digital twin technology underscore its transformative journey. Born from necessity, nurtured by progress, and perfected through collaboration, digital twins have arrived at the forefront of technological advancement. As history has demonstrated, with the convergence of technology, it stands ready to reshape yet another era, much like it transformed those before.

1.3   Key Components and Structure

To truly appreciate the elegance of digital twin technology, one must delve into its architecture—the building blocks that transform raw data into insightful applications. Imagine constructing a house without understanding the significance of its architectural elements. You'll quickly realize that before we paint the walls or furnish the rooms, we must ensure the foundations and framework are impeccable. Similarly, in digital twins, it is the underlying components that determine their power and utility.

Let us embark on a journey through the essential components of a digital twin and the ingenious ways these elements come together to form a cohesive whole.

- **The Physical Entity**

At the heart of any digital twin lies its physical counterpart—the object, system, or process it seeks to emulate. From colossal engines and delicate medical devices to sprawling cityscapes, these physical entities provide the foundation upon which digital twins are constructed. It is their characteristics and behaviors that digital twins mirror, enabling users to interact with a full-scale replica in the digital realm.

Take, for example, a complex manufacturing assembly line. This tangible system operates through numerous moving parts and intricate dynamics. The digital twin's task is to capture the nuances of this physical entity, creating a platform that mimics performance and predicts outcomes with uncanny fidelity. The physical entity thus becomes a source of data, providing the lifeblood that animates its digital twin.

- **The Digital Representation**

  Think of this as the soul of the digital twin, a sophisticated virtual construct that embodies its physical partner. This digital version incorporates a myriad of elements, ranging from 3D architectural models to intricate datasets derived from the physical world. The finesse of this digital representation is paramount; it needs to not only visualize but also replicate the functional aspects with precision.

  Consider the digital twin of a bridge. Not only is an accurate 3D image vital for visualization, but it must also simulate stress factors, temperature variations, and wear over time. These complex models allow engineers to foresee structural fatigue or potential cracks through what are otherwise visu-

11

alizations that are beyond the surface. Historical
data and patterns are vital to refine these models
and augment their predictive prowess.

- **The Data Connection**

  The intelligence of digital twins thrives on data,
  and therein lies the critical connection—the
  robust, seamless, and constant flow of information
  between the physical entity and its digital
  reflection.   Through sensors, IoT devices, and
  communication networks, data is gathered,
  transmitted, and assimilated in real-time.

  Imagine a smart wind farm, where windswept turbines communicate live performance data to their
  corresponding digital twins. Each turbine's twin is
  constantly updated with metrics such as rotational
  speed, air temperature, and blade angles, among
  others. This relentless data influx allows these digital constructs to perform in-depth analyses, recognizing patterns invisibly weaving through operational data and enhancing decision-making capabilities.

- **Analytical Capabilities**

  Embedded within every digital twin is a robust
  analytical engine—a cerebral core that processes
  and interprets incoming data.   These advanced
  analytical capabilities enable the digital twin to
  transform streams of information into actionable
  insights, simulating outcomes or diagnosing
  anomalies.

  An apt parallel can be drawn with the automotive
  industry's use of digital twins. Here, data-driven
  analytics allow virtual car models to adapt

dynamically, testing various driving conditions, safety scenarios, and even hypothetical design alterations. The analytics at play detect minute patterns, refining the vehicle without physically altering the prototype, a luxury prior generations couldn't afford.

- **Visualization Interface**

  Embodied in every digital twin is an intuitive interface that renders complex data into visually comprehensible and interactive formats. Such interfaces act as the portal through which users can explore and manipulate their digital twins, a crucial tool in bridging gaps between human perception and complex digital information.

  Take the energy sector, for instance. Plant managers utilize digital twins with dashboards showcasing energy flows, efficiency metrics, and predictive maintenance schedules. These interfaces are not only comprehensive but also customizable, enabling stakeholders to make informed decisions, mitigate risks, and optimize performance at a glance.

- **Control and Automation**

  The pinnacle of digital twin utility lies in its ability to not just simulate, but to actively influence real-world outcomes. Elements of control and automation transform the digital twin from a passive entity into an agent of change, equipped to instruct its physical counterpart toward optimized functioning.

  In automated warehouses, digital twins can issue commands to robotic systems for smarter task

13

allocation, routing, and inventory management. This results in faster, more efficient processes without human intervention—a glimpse into a future steered by digital intelligence.

- **Feedback Loop**

    Finally, the feedback loop in a digital twin fosters continuous improvement and learning. Unlike static models, digital twins evolve in tandem with their physical entities, influenced by new data and results. As they cycle through data collection, analysis, visualization, and adjustment, digital twins enhance their accuracy and predictive prowess.

    A poignant illustration lies within healthcare. Personalized digital twins of patients allow doctors to simulate treatments and observe outcomes. This cycle of testing and refinement via simulated feedback can lead to customized healthcare solutions, improving efficacy while minimizing adverse effects.

In essence, the architecture of digital twins reflects a profound interplay of these components, resulting in a synergy that amplifies the potential of each. By combining physical realism with digital adaptability, analytics with automation, and interfaces with intuition, digital twins become far more than a sum of their parts—a living, breathing tapestry of the virtual and the real.

As our understanding of digital twins continues to deepen, and the components evolve, we are poised to witness a renaissance of innovation across industries. The capability to not only mirror the real world but improve and redefine it marks the threshold of a digitally integrated future. Digital twins exemplify how a meticulous synergy of structure and creativity can shape tomorrow's answers to today's questions, one byte at a time.

1.4 Significance in Modern Technology

In the grand orchestra of modern technology, digital twin technology plays a role not unlike a virtuoso performer, harmonizing with other innovations to create a symphony of progress. It is a testament to human ingenuity—an innovative confluence that amplifies our ability to comprehend, control, and optimize the world around us. To truly grasp its significance, we must explore how digital twins integrate with contemporary technological paradigms, transforming industries and redefining the boundaries of possibility.

Digital twins are spearheading advancements across an array of fields, offering unprecedented precision in monitoring, simulation, and optimization. Consider the world of smart manufacturing, where efficiency and agility are not merely preferences but imperatives. Factories powered by digital twins can predict machine failures, streamline production processes through simulation, and reduce waste by optimizing resource allocation. The result is the rise of Industry 4.0— a networked ecosystem where every element of production is digitally intertwined with impeccable accuracy.

One illustrative example is Siemens, a powerhouse of industrial automation, which employs digital twins to simulate and refine its manufacturing processes. Through real-time data and predictive capabilities, Siemens not only improves operational efficiency but also significantly shortens product development cycles, bringing innovations to market faster than ever before.

In the burgeoning field of smart cities, digital twins stand at the forefront of urban innovation. As the global population migrates increasingly to urban settings, managing the complexity of cities becomes a pressing challenge. Here, digital twins offer municipal planners a virtual canvas where they can model infrastructure, visualize energy consumption, and anticipate traffic patterns. By engaging in this digital mimicry, cities can allocate resources efficiently, enhance public safety, and improve citizens' quality of life.

Take Singapore, an exemplar of digital twin implementation. The city-state uses a comprehensive digital twin model to oversee urban development, optimize utilities, and predict environmental impacts. By layering data from transportation, utilities, and demographics, Singapore's urban planners visualize and test potential interventions long before physical changes are executed, a testament to the power of foresight in a rapidly evolving urban landscape.

Healthcare technology, another sphere where precision is paramount, finds a valuable ally in digital twins. Personalized patient care can benefit dramatically from precise digital replicas that simulate the impacts of treatment paths. Imagine a cardiac surgeon who, before performing a delicate procedure, can rehearse on a digital twin of the patient's heart—honed from real-time data and historical health records. This capability not only heightens the success rate of medical interventions but also personalizes treatment to levels previously deemed unattainable.

In energy management, digital twins are revolutionizing how we conceptualize and manage sustainability.

The energy sector, rife with complexity, requires intricate monitoring and optimization to fuel a future characterized by renewable resources and minimized carbon footprints. Consider wind farms employing digital twins to ensure optimal blade positioning based on real-time meteorological data; the result is maximized energy capture with minimal wear, a win-win for efficiency and longevity.

Beyond these tangible applications, digital twins hold philosophical significance, illustrating humankind's quest to merge reality with virtuality. As sensors and IoT devices proliferate, the boundary between the digital and the physical begins to blur, prompting profound questions about how we conceptualize existence, interaction, and understanding. Through digital twins, we embark on a profound journey toward a digital globalization, where borders dissolve into pixels, and barriers fall as quickly as they are imagined.

The coupling of digital twins with artificial intelligence further expands their potential, enabling systems that learn, adapt, and self-optimize. This profound synergy creates an environment where not only do digital twins reflect physical reality, but they also influence it, driving innovations that are as reactive as they are preemptive. Consider autonomous vehicles that integrate digital twin technology with AI, learning from every drive to become safer, more efficient, and more proficient over time.

Digital twins also democratize access to advanced technology, lowering barriers for smaller enterprises traditionally edged out by titans of industry. In entrepreneurship and innovation, start-ups harness digital twins to model and refine products cost-effectively, testing hypotheses in a virtual sandbox free from the constraints of capital-intensive physical prototypes.   This democratization fosters creativity and diversity, engendering a vibrant ecosystem of possibilities previously reserved for established players.

The educational field, a testament to the transcendent power of knowledge, finds its paradigms reshaped through digital twins.   Consider classrooms where complex phenomena are not only described but experienced. Students in a biology class could observe cellular processes not as static illustrations but as dynamic interactions within a digital twin, seamlessly blending theory with reality.

One might wonder if there is a catch—a specter of dependence or a risk embedded within the convenience offered by digital twins. As with any transformative technology, challenges loom. Data privacy, security, and ethical considerations must navigate the intricate balance between technological advancement and societal values. The delicate dance requires vigilance, responsibility, and a forward-thinking ethos to ensure that progress does not outpace prudence.

In surveying the significance of digital twin technology, one uncovers a panorama where the future is shaped not merely by human hands, but by the digital reflections they create. These reflections offer clarity and insight, enabling us to view our world from a fresher perspective. As virtual and physical realities converge, the possibilities unroll before us like an uncharted map—rich in promise, and bound only by the limits of our imagination.

Indeed, our engagement with digital twins is a narrative not just of technological marvels but of human ambition and creativity, how we have sculpted a tool that enriches and extends our ability to innovate. As digital twins become embedded in the pulse of technology, they embody not only the sophisticated artifice of our current age but also the seeds of transformation for what lies ahead—a dance across the digital divide, a symphony conducted in code and concrete.

1.5   Common Misconceptions

As with any burgeoning technology, digital twins find themselves enshrouded in myths and misunderstandings— specters of confusion mingling with truth, often muddying the waters of public perception. Just as folklore crafts mythical creatures from shadows and whispers, the ambiguity surrounding digital twins can stem from a mix of overambition, oversimplification, or plain misunderstanding. It is time to set the record straight, dispelling these myths to foster a clearer understanding of the digital twin phenomenon.

Myth 1: Digital Twins Are Merely 3D Models

Picture a digital twin as nothing more than a detailed 3D model, akin to a Photoshop rendering or a CAD diagram. This misconception, albeit popular, fails to recognize the depth and dynamism inherent in digital twins. While visualization is a component, digital twins extend far beyond mere aesthetics. They unite vast arrays of data, real-time monitoring, and predictive analytics, creating an interactive, functional equivalent of the physical entity they represent.

Imagine an orchestra—while the conductor can visualize a score, it is the symphony of instruments, the flow of melodies and harmonies, that transforms notes into music. Similarly, while a 3D model captures the static essence, digital twins embody the living, breathing orchestra of data, interaction, and analytics that replay reality in all its complexity.

Myth 2: Digital Twins Only Apply to Large-Scale Industrial Projects

The thought that digital twins are constrained to the vast, cavernous halls of industry giants—factories, skyscrapers, or sprawling power plants—is a limitation imposed by imagination, not by technology. Digital twins are versatile shapeshifters, adaptable to diverse contexts, from the individual scale of personal health monitoring to massive infrastructure undertakings.

Consider the world of sports, where athletes leverage digital twins to optimize performance. A cyclist dons sensors that transmit data to their digital doppelgänger, which analyzes and suggests enhancements in posture or power output. This demonstrates digital twins' capacity to operate not just at colossal scales but at personal levels, where even miniscule improvements yield tangible benefits.

Myth 3: Digital Twins Are Self-Sufficient and Fully Autonomous

To envision digital twins as independent entities performing prodigious feats unaided is a misconception akin to mistaking a robot for a sentient being. While digital twins are powerful, they require human input, interpretation, and guidance. Picture them as exceptional tools—highly sophisticated wrenches or microscopes—functioning at peak performance when wielded by knowledgeable hands.

The functions of a digital twin—monitoring, simulation, prediction—are augmented by human oversight, wherein the insights gleaned are transformed into actionable strategies. Rather than being autonomous solutions, digital twins are collaborators in innovation, enhancing human ability to strategize, analyze, and resolve.

Myth 4: Digital Twins Eliminate All Risk

In a world fond of attributing miraculous powers to the digital realm, it can be tempting to view digital twins as infallible guardians of efficiency and certainty. However, assuming they eradicate all risk and uncertainty is as misguided as expecting a meteorologist to banish inclement weather. Digital twins enhance predictive and preventative measures, yet remain subject to the chaos of real-world variables.

Imagine a digital twin predicting machinery wear-and-tear in a manufacturing plant. While it offers invaluable foresight, variables such as unexpected material defects or supply chain disruptions may still trigger anomalies. Embracing digital twins means embracing a tool that mitigates risk, not one that abolishes it; they are a beacon of preparedness navigating the unpredictable tides of reality.

Myth 5: Implementing Digital Twins is Quick and Simple

While the allure of digital twins as a panacea for complex problems is undeniable, realizing their potential is neither instantaneous nor simple. Implementation demands a concerted effort—refining processes, integrating systems, and continuous data management.

Take the aviation industry, where developing a cohesive digital twin requires harmonizing diverse data streams from sensors, maintenance logs, and flight data—each element necessitating careful calibration and integration to form a coherent whole. The journey toward full-scale digital twin implementation reflects a marathon, not a sprint, with progress marked by continuous refinement and strategic foresight.

Myth 6: Digital Twins Are a Passing Fad

A skepticism permeates technological evolution—
the notion that digital twins belong to the realm of
transient trends, destined to fade like forgotten memes.
Contrarily, the principles underpinning digital twin
technology draw on enduring needs for simulation,
optimization, and data-informed decisions.

This misconception overlooks the monumental
shifts driven by digital twins across industries—
transformations in urban planning, revolutionizing
healthcare, and advancing precision manufacturing.
Far from fleeting, digital twins are at the vanguard
of innovation, embodying the future state of systems
integration, intelligent design, and predictive command.

The goal of challenging these misconceptions is not to
dampen enthusiasm or funnel skepticism, but to illuminate the realities of digital twins—their potential, boundaries, and nuanced roles they play in technology's vast
orchestra. Acknowledging these truths equips us with
the insight to wield digital twins most effectively, understanding them not as standalone saviors but as partners
on the journey of innovation.

As we forge onward, shedding assumptions and embracing clarity, the story of digital twins deepens—a narrative rooted not in mystique but in mastery. It is a call to
see beyond the myths and into the myriad facets where
digital twins flourish, transcending simplicity to become
architects of a future—a future where myths give way to
mastery, and technology marries imagination, crafting a
tapestry of possibilities.

Chapter 2

The Origins and Evolution of Digital Twins

Digital twins originated from early efforts in simulation and modeling, gaining formal recognition through NASA's application in space missions to enhance system reliability. This concept gradually extended to various industries, including manufacturing and infrastructure, where it spurred innovation. Technological advancements, such as increased computing power and the integration of IoT, have been pivotal in their evolution. This chapter explores the journey of digital twin technology from specialized beginnings to mainstream adoption, highlighting its transformative potential in modern industry applications.

2.1 Roots in Simulation and Modeling

Welcome to the realm of simulation and modeling, where reality blurs into possibility, and imagination intertwines with logic to produce technological marvels. The concept of digital twins did not spontaneously materialize from the ether; rather, it is deeply rooted in centuries of human endeavor to simulate the world around us, allowing us to predict, control, and innovate with remarkable precision.

The story of simulation begins long before the advent of modern computers. Ancient engineers and mathematicians used rudimentary models—scaled-down representations of large structures—to test hypotheses and solve problems. The Great Pyramid of Giza and the aqueducts of Rome stand testament to the calculative prowess and model-based planning of civilizations that laid history's foundational stones.

Fast forward a few millennia, and the art of modeling takes a significant leap forward with the introduction of mathematical concepts. In the 17th century, the dawn of calculus opened new horizons for simulating natural phenomena, challenging scientists to think of the world in terms of equations and experiments. Isaac Newton's laws of motion and calculus were revolutionary tools that allowed humans to predict planetary movements and navigate the cosmos with newfound confidence.

The Industrial Revolution marked another turning point, where models transcended stone to fuel innovation during an era of mechanization and growth. Engineers used scale models to design steam engines and bridge structures, optimizing designs while minimizing risk. With each model, humans honed their ability to simulate the tactile world into abstract representations that promised further understanding.

While these early efforts laid the groundwork, the 20th century catapulted simulation and modeling into a new dimension—digitization. The advent of computers transformed mere models into complex simulations. Herein lies a crucial development: the ability to simulate systems through digital computation. This shift revolutionized industries, allowing for precise design, testing, and refinement previously considered a pipedream.

Consider the aerospace industry, where flight simulators emerged as an ingenious solution to the inherent dangers of early aviation. Allowing pilots to experience authentic conditions within a controlled setting, these simulators pioneered virtual environments capable of replicating the unforgiving sky. As technology evolved, so did the simulators' precision, laying a direct path towards the intricate digital twins of today.

Simulations expanded beyond airplanes. They influenced nuclear engineering, medicine, and automobile industries. In automotive testing, simulation platforms enabled engineers to virtually test vehicle dynamics and safety, reducing costly prototypes and accelerating innovation. As a critical leap, simulations transformed into engines of discovery—ventures into uncharted territories translating ideas into tangible outcomes.

The bridge from pure simulation to the more sophisticated concept of digital twins involved two significant developments. First, the refinement of computer-aided design (CAD) software. CAD permitted not just visualization but also manipulation of designs, embracing an intricate interaction between the conceptual and operational realms. Engineers could draft intricate details on virtual canvases, seeing on-screen every bend and turn as if it were steel or aluminum.

Second, integrating simulation with real-time data emerged as a revolutionary step. As sensors became more sophisticated, simulations could no longer be isolated constructs—they needed to evolve, reaching out to their real-world counterparts. This integration laid the germ for digital twins, where data upon data

breathed life into models, shattering static boundaries
with dynamic representation.

Financial sectors, too, embraced simulation-driven
decisions.   Financial modeling, though less tangible,
wielded simulations to explore numerous market
scenarios, enabling stakeholders to steer investments
with calculated foresight. Whether simulating market
fluctuations or global events, these models laid the
bedrock for pivotal economic decisions.

The burgeoning field of computational science further
bolstered the role of simulation and modeling. Scientists
could now create simulations of previously impercepti-
ble phenomena—from molecular interactions dictating
chemical reactions to cosmic events sculpting galaxies.
Through advanced algorithms, these simulations
pushed the limits of human understanding.

As we stride further into a digital world, it is clear that
simulation and modeling continue to be a profound axis
around which modern advancements revolve. Their evolution into digital twins extends from a rich heritage of
thinking beyond the tangible—of daring to replicate and
reimagine what it means to understand a system holistically.

In the educational sector, learners explore physics
concepts through simulated labs, conducting experiments without glass flasks or chemical hazards. Such
platforms brim with potential, democratizing access to
cutting-edge science and encouraging a new wave of
curiosity and discovery.

In reflecting on the roots of simulation and modeling,
one discerns a narrative shadowing technology with
threads of human ingenuity. From simple scale models
and mathematical conjectures to sophisticated digital
environments, this lineage emphasizes an enduring

truth: our propensity to know and control the world is fueled by our ability to create and simulate.

As the seeds of history cultivate the digital twins of today, they remind us that simulation and modeling are more than conceptual tools; they are the living architecture of progress, the frameworks upon which we continue to construct the future—a simulated journey that reveals, innovates, and evolves across time. Through their legacy, digital twins become more than twins; they are symbiotic siblings nurturing the continual evolution of technology in tandem with our ever-expanding understanding of the universe.

2.2 The NASA Connection

In technological innovation, few organizations are as entwined with the concept of exploration and pushing boundaries as NASA. From its inaugural leaps towards the cosmos to its contemporary endeavors unraveling the mysteries of Mars, NASA's narrative is one punctuated by audacity and intellect in equal measure. Nestled within the chronicles of its storied past lies a pivotal concept that helped sculpt modern engineering and technology: the digital twin.

To understand this connection, let us journey back to the 1960s—a time when humankind first cast its eyes skyward with a genuine intent to touch the heavens. The Apollo program, a hallmark of ingenuity and daring, is well-remembered for placing astronauts on the lunar surface. Yet, behind this glamour lay the monumental complexity of ensuring reliability and safety for missions on the brink of possibility. It is here that digital twins find their conceptual genesis.

NASA faced an intimidating challenge: executing

missions of enormous complexity where the margin
for error was microscopic.   As missions ventured
beyond terrestrial constraints, real-time simulation and
modeling, as explored earlier, proved indispensable.
NASA sought to virtualize spacecraft systems, creating
simulations that acted as silent sentinels, constantly
reflecting and predicting the behavior of these systems
in space. These proto-digital twins enabled engineers to
monitor system variables and diagnose issues without
direct physical interaction—crucial when dealing with
vessels enroute to the Moon.

A prime example of the impact of these early digital
twins can be found in the Apollo 13 mission. Famously
dubbed a "successful failure," Apollo 13 encountered a
life-threatening crisis when an oxygen tank exploded. In
the void of space, astronauts James Lovell, Jack Swigert,
and Fred Haise faced daunting odds. NASA's ground
control harnessed the virtual replicas—digital twins,
albeit not yet called as such—to model, assess, and
implement life-saving strategies. Through simulations
reflecting ship conditions, they meticulously engineered
the famous slingshot maneuver that returned the
crew safely to Earth—a testament to the pragmatic
application of twin-like practices.

The progression from simulation to a more formal
digital twin concept occurred during the shift from
Apollo to subsequent ambitious ventures like the
Space Shuttle program.   Here, NASA redefined
engineering practices, weaving intricate synergies
between computers and physical systems. The Shuttle's
complexity demanded thorough simulation but of
a nature more integrated and intelligent than past
efforts. An evolution unfolded: from isolated models
to comprehensive virtual counterparts capable of
mimicking real-time states—a vision intrinsic to the

digital twin philosophy.

In parallel, NASA's journey illuminated the importance of data. Each byte collected from spacecraft instruments and mission telemetry contributed to building a digital consciousness. These data points were the neurons in the brains of digital twins, fostering real-time convergence between the space-borne and the earthbound. As missions reached further—Voyager carving paths through celestial echoes, and satellites tracing orbits around our distant planetary neighbors—the role of data-driven understanding abounded.

The evolution of digital twins alongside NASA's technological advancements offers lessons that transcend space exploration. For instance, the meticulous calibration of navigational models demonstrated during the Shuttle program laid groundwork representative of operational precision applicable across industries today. It became clear that the power of digital twins lies not simply in replication but in fostering an agile thinking framework—a system alert to deviations, capable of predictive foresight.

As decades progressed, NASA continued pioneering digital twin applications in domains as diverse as the exploration of Mars and advancements in aerodynamics. The Mars Rover programs—Curiosity, Spirit, and Opportunity—each exemplified twin concepts by transforming Martian data into actionable insights. Ground-based twins mirrored rover operations, enabling scientists to rehearse movements, preempt technical woes, and simulate environmental interactions thousands of miles from where crimson dust swirled.

Moreover, NASA's aeronautics research centers developed digital twins that transformed the landscape of aviation. In pursuit of enhanced air travel safety

and efficiency, attitudes shifted from reactive crisis
management to proactive maintenance methodologies.
Digital twins capable of simulating and predicting
aviation component wear were instituted, echoing
Apollo 13's legacy of resilience—a legacy emergent
from necessity, fostered by ingenuity.

Drawing parallels between NASA's pioneering digital
twin efforts and contemporary industry, one witnesses a
shared journey from complexity to clarity. As industries
harness twin technology, the narrative of NASA's role
becomes a beacon—a reminder that extraordinary
achievements arise from understanding not merely the
final frontier but integrating the digital and physical
across every facet of existence. NASA exemplifies the
paradigm of innovation, where digital twins—although
born from celestial dreams—promised to ground
humanity's endeavors with the gravity of foresight.

As we stand on the edge of the digital age, the trajectory
NASA embarked upon invites reflection on the power
of convergence. The agency's holistic embrace of data,
evolutionary modeling techniques, and twin-like adaptations underscores the possibility inherent in collaboration: a partnership between human curiosity and digital
intimacy.

In the incandescence of today's technology, where
digital twins play indispensable roles from urban
planning to personalized medicine, the shields of
learning battered into shape by NASA's celestial
voyages stand vivid, guiding the path. Herein lies
the NASA connection—a symphonic exploration of
virtuality and reality seamlessly intertwined, enriching
our grasp of the universe, one digital model at a time.
Through the legacy of space-bound aspirations, we
witness a vivid portrayal of the future graced by the
wisdom of collaboration across distances both cosmic

and corporate, all birthed from the quest to understand that which lies beyond the stars.

2.3 Industrial Adoption and Innovation

If digital twins were players in a grand technological saga, the industrial sector would surely be their bustling stage. As sensors shrugged off bulkiness for elegance and data became the lingua franca of progress, industries across the globe began to recognize the symbiotic allure of digital twins. Defined by their capacity to infuse operations with intelligence, agility, and insight, digital twins have ushered in a new era—one where the tangible and the digital dance in harmony, driving unprecedented innovation.

Let's embark on a journey through the kaleidoscope of industrial adoption, where the seeds of digital twin technology have blossomed into vibrant orchards of innovation.

Manufacturing: The Digital Renaissance

The manufacturing industry—a realm traditionally dominated by towering machines and whirring assembly lines—found in digital twins a guide from the predictable to the prognostic. Here, digital twins bestowed manufacturers with newfound clairvoyance: the ability to predict equipment failures, optimize production schedules, and reduce downtime. The result? An industrial renaissance, characterized by factories that hum with optimized efficiency.

Take the automotive industry, where giants like Toyota have embraced digital twins to revolutionize vehicle design and production. By simulating diverse manufacturing processes, they unraveled the complexities of assembly, welding, and painting—far before the smell of engine oil permeates the air. These virtual simulations afford engineers the luxury of preemptive troubleshooting, precluding issues before any bolt is tightened or panel is painted.

In aerospace, the stakes are sky-high. Aircraft manufacturers like Boeing utilize digital twins to simulate aerodynamics, electrical systems, and cabin layouts long before cockpit windows herald blue skies. Beyond mechanical proficiency, digital twins extend lifelines to safety: simulating potential failures, stress-testing components, and monitoring real-time analytics during flights to ensure safety glides tranquilly through the skies.

Energy and Utilities: Powering Precision

The energy sector, infused with the dual mandates of sustainability and efficiency, found in digital twins a partner adept at reconciling these goals. These digital sorcerers stood ready to optimize energy grids, monitor renewable energy farms, and simulate the ebb and flow of power distribution—a wizardry entwined with daily demands.

Consider the wind energy industry where digital twins oversee an array of turbines dotting the landscapes, each tasked with converting zephyrs into kilowatts. By simulating wind patterns, operational stresses, and maintenance needs, digital twins reduce wear and tear on turbines, ensuring that they meet the daily embrace of wind with poise. This venture into the wind-driven future transcends energy production—it's a leap into the heart of climate-conscious praxis.

In oil and gas, digital twins provide clarity amid the murky depths of exploration. Companies like BP employ them to simulate the intricate geology of oil reservoirs, permitting cautious drilling that mitigates environmental impact. Through digital doubles of drilling operations and infrastructure, companies translate past experiences into predictive insights, ensuring that nature's depths yield returns responsibly.

Urban Infrastructure: The Blueprint of Tomorrow

Our cities—complex tapestries of cement, transit networks, and human lives—offer a singular stage for digital twin intervention. Urban planners, equipped with these digital maestros, simulate entire neighborhoods, predicting their evolution and optimizing functionality long before the first slab is laid.

The City of London draws upon digital twins to manage and predict urban growth—a digital tapestry forecasting energy consumption, population density, and transportation dynamics. They're employed to visualize and simulate potential infrastructure changes, effortlessly choreographing seamless daily commutes, waste management, and utility provision. By reflecting a digital twin vision, Londoners navigate cities that breathe with intelligent efficiency.

Transportation infrastructure, like railways and roadways, likewise finds digital twins as invaluable allies in transforming traditional operations into streamlined spectacles. Trains powered by the United Kingdom's Network Rail project whisk passengers across landscapes, guided by digital twins that simulate schedules and track conditions, optimizing journeys for safety and punctuality.

Healthcare: The Personalized Revolution

In the domain of healthcare, digital twins are igniting a paradigm shift from generic treatment approaches to-

ward the hallowed realm of personalization. Hospitals
and clinics utilize patient-specific digital twins—vivid
replicas united with medical data streams—to simulate
disease progression, test potential treatments, and customize interventions.

Picture a digital twin of the human heart, where
cardiologists model blood flow and ventricular function,
testing the impact of medications and predicting
potential cardiac events. The British Heart Foundation
supports such groundbreaking research, previewing a
future where digital twins tailor treatments as unique
as the DNA of the patients they replicate.

Beyond patients, hospital operations embrace these
virtual companions to optimize facility management—
from ensuring energy-efficient buildings to predicting
medical equipment needs and staffing schedules,
transforming patient care from a routine to a precisely
orchestrated symphony.

Supply Chain: The Connectivity Matrix

The intricacies of supply chains, moving goods across
countries and continents, are historically fraught with
complexity and risk. Here, digital twins take the form
of conductors, harmonizing disparate elements into cohesive networks. By simulating supply chain scenarios,
companies foresee interruptions, optimize routes, and
anticipate market fluctuations.

Technology giants like Amazon leverage digital twins
to monitor their vast distribution networks, simulating
inventory flows and delivery pathways, ensuring that
packages arrive timely and efficiently. This capability
is not mere connectivity—it's a dynamic relationship
that translates data into actionable strategies, enhancing
consumer satisfaction across the globe.

Across these diverse sectors, digital twins are not mere spectators; they are transformative agents driving the lexicon of 21st-century industry. What began in the annals of NASA and aerospace has permeated into the fabric of global innovation, proving that when digital mirrors reality, industries become poised to write stories where potential is unbounded and efficiency is redefined.

As industries continue to integrate digital twins into their ecosystems, we draw close to an era where innovation is not just imagined but lived—an era where industrial adoption catalyzes a connate dance between digital intelligence and human creativity, offering a tantalizing glimpse of the potential world to come. Through this burgeoning convergence, digital twins pave pathways through industry that are as exhilarating as they are essential, transforming innovation from aspiration into existence.

2.4 Technological Advances Enabling Growth

As we explore the dynamic world of digital twins, it becomes evident that their proliferation rests upon the shoulders of modern technological advancements—each a stepping stone heralding growth and opportunity. The past few decades have witnessed a revolution in computing, data analytics, and connectivity, creating a fertile landscape for digital twins to flourish and redefine industries. Let's navigate this terrain, examining the technological forces that have propelled digital twins from niche curiosities to essential elements of contemporary innovation.

- **Computing Power: The Digital Dynamo**

The evolution of digital twins is intimately tied to
the rise of computing power—a dynamic akin to
comparing a horse-drawn cart to the sleek speed
of a modern jetliner. Back in the 1960s, computing
was colossal and cumbersome, yet today's devices
fit snugly in our pockets, sporting computational
prowess that outperforms eyesore mainframes of
yore.

Consider the birth of Moore's Law, predictively
doubling transistors on microchips every two
years—an insight that has held remarkably true.
This exponential growth transformed computing
from exclusive labyrinths of academia and
government into a democratized cornerstone
of business and innovation. Sophisticated
simulations and real-time data processing, once
pipe dreams, are now the province of personal
computers and cloud-based infrastructures.

With this newfound power, digital twins emulate
complex systems at unprecedented scales. IBM
Watson, for instance, harnesses computational
advances to deliver healthcare solutions, analyzing
vast data sets to create personalized patient digital
twins—a marvel of precision and potential.
As processing capabilities further evolve, the
sophistication of digital twins will continue
to escalate in tandem, emboldening predictive
analytics and intelligent decision-making.

- **Data Analytics: Decoding the Deluge**

Imagine the digital universe as a vast and boundless library. Each byte, dataset, or document represents an opportunity to glean insight from the
barrage of information now woven into our daily
lives. Enter data analytics—the discerning librar-

ian guiding us through a sea of information, making sense of chaos with precision and clarity.

As digital ecosystems expanded, data analytics matured from primitive databases into complex systems capable of mining vast troves of structured and unstructured data. With advances in machine learning algorithms, these systems now detect patterns and extract valuable insights from torrents of information—an indispensable capability for digital twins relying on real-time data to model, predict, and refine.

Take predictive maintenance, where industrial giants utilize data analytics to empower digital twins. By sifting through streams of sensor data, digital twins of machinery and equipment anticipate failures before they occur—ensuring reliability and continuous operation through proactive maintenance strategies.

- **The Rise of IoT: Sensors in Symphony**

  Empower the world with sensors, and reality transforms into a digital tapestry alive with information, ripe for reflection and manipulation. This premise forms the core of the Internet of Things (IoT), where a host of interconnected devices share data, enriching digital twins with context and connectivity.

  This sensor symphony infuses digital twins with precise, real-time information that keeps them accurate and up-to-date—a live reflection of the world they model. For instance, digital twins of smart buildings use IoT devices to monitor energy consumption, adapt to changing conditions, and optimize comfort for occupants—issuing profound insights into resource use and sustainability.

The trajectory of IoT ensures that digital twins become increasingly granular, modeling systems down to individual components and interactions. As 5G connectivity emerges, the speed and volume of data exchanged will grow exponentially, fueling even more sophisticated digital twin enterprises.

- **Cloud Computing: The Infrastructure Engine**

Before the era of cloud computing, digital twins operated within constraints, limited by the physical capacity of hardware and silos of information. The advent of cloud architectures reshaped this landscape, offering infinite scalability, storage, and computational resources— a paradigm shift that liberated digital twins from prior confines.

Companies like Amazon Web Services (AWS) and Microsoft Azure offer platforms that allow the creation, deployment, and management of digital twins across global infrastructures. Whether a start-up crafting a digital representation of a new product or an enterprise modeling global supply chains, the cloud offers a limitless arena where twin ecosystems can expand and evolve.

This infrastructure empowers collaborations that transcend borders, inviting innovation and insight-sharing in spaces previously restricted by geography or capital. An exciting byproduct of this shift is the potential for smaller enterprises to access and leverage powerful technologies once reserved for industry titans.

- **Artificial Intelligence: Intellect in the Machine**

Where traditional simulations once mirrored the present, artificial intelligence imbues digital twins with intellect—a conscious evolution from passive reflection to proactive engagement. Machine learning and deep learning offer digital twins the ability to analyze past performance, predict future trends, and adapt intelligently to emerging scenarios.

Imagine autonomous vehicles, where digital twins powered by AI enhance navigation, predict road conditions, and adapt driving strategies in real-time. Companies like Tesla leverage AI-powered digital twins to improve vehicle safety and performance, creating a cascade of benefits that ripple through both innovation and consumer satisfaction.

AI helps digital twins transcend simple replication, crafting intricate ecosystems that balance analytics with action. This advancement ensures that digital twins not only model current states but offer foresight and agility—a transformative progression toward true system intelligence.

- **Cybersecurity: The Trustworthy Guardian**

  As digital twins expand and evolve, the specter of cyber threats looms large, where breaches could compromise sensitive data and critical systems. Cybersecurity—once an afterthought—is now a paramount consideration in ensuring the integrity and trustworthiness of digital twin ecosystems.

  Technological advances in encryption, identity management, and threat detection enhance the security portfolio of digital twins, ensuring they remain resilient against malicious disruptions. Initiatives like blockchain technology offer transparency and traceability, safeguarding transactions and augmenting digital twin reliability in industries like finance and healthcare.

The intersection of cybersecurity and digital twins represents the imperative to protect investments and data—an essential component of fostering trust and safeguarding technological growth.

As the symphony of technological advancements plays on, the crescendo guiding digital twins continues to harmonize, each innovation resonating with the next. The convergence of computing power, data analytics, IoT, cloud computing, artificial intelligence, and cybersecurity creates a potent brew—an elixir of progress empowering digital twins with unprecedented potential.

This harmonious synergy fuels growth across industries, catalyzing developments that redefine efficiency, innovation, and resilience. As we stand at the frontier of the digital age, the growth trajectory of digital twins offers tantalizing glimpses of what lies ahead—an era where technology and creativity converge, crafting a world infused with knowledge, insight, and possibility. Through continued collaboration and foresight, digital twins will undoubtedly remain an indelible force, woven intricately into the fabric of future industry.

2.5   Transition to Mainstream Use

Every technological innovation experiences a moment of reckoning—a transition from the fringes of experimentation to the heart of mainstream consciousness. For digital twins, this moment has arrived in a flourish, as they shift from specialized realms into diverse industries, defining the modern technological paradigm. The journey has been one of adaptation, innovation, and, crucially, integration into the fabric of everyday operations.

Let us chart this remarkable trajectory, understanding how digital twins have made the leap from concept to commonplace, reshaping landscapes across sectors.

- **The Rise of Awareness and Acceptance**

  In the early stages of their development, digital twins were viewed as the domain of deep-pocketed industrial giants—an advanced tool accessible only through significant investment and expertise. However, as success stories emerged and barriers to entry lowered, awareness and acceptance soared.

  This rise can be traced to key demonstrations of digital twin potential. Industries witnessing tangible benefits through practical implementations began to embrace the technology with fervor. Case studies proliferated, highlighting how digital twins reduced costs, increased efficiency, and bolstered resilience—an enticing prospect for stakeholders.

  Conferences, symposiums, and white papers became platforms showcasing digital twin miraculousness, engendering curiosity. What was once niche now stood poised at the forefront of innovation, heralding opportunities for sectors ranging from healthcare to education.

- **Market Expansion: From Pioneers to Pervasive Use**

  The expansion of digital twin technology into mainstream use paralleled the technology penetrating new markets, adapting to ecosystems beyond its original aerospace and manufacturing confines. Sectors like agriculture, retail, and

41

logistics began exploring digital twin opportunities, recognizing their potential to optimize and transform operations.

Consider agriculture, where digital twins now model crop health, predict yield variations, and simulate environmental impacts. Modern farms leverage digital twins to preemptively respond to pestilence, drought, or natural shifts, aligning ancient cultivation with cutting-edge precision.

Retail and e-commerce also embrace digital twin models to simulate consumer behavior, streamline supply chains, and personalize shopping experiences. Retail juggernauts like Walmart use digital twins to recreate store layouts on virtual platforms, fine-tuning customer journey strategies to enhance engagement and satisfaction.

- **Technological Enablers: Democratizing Access**

  As previously discussed, technological advancements have paved a wider path for digital twins, propelling them from exclusivity toward accessibility. The democratization of computing power, proliferation of IoT devices, and availability of cloud platforms empower organizations of all sizes to adopt digital twin technology without necessitating prohibitive investment.

  Cloud-based solutions offer businesses scalable infrastructure and tools to develop and manage digital twins, levelling the playing field for start-ups and small enterprises. The rise of Software as a Service (SaaS) and digital twin platforms as a service (DTaaS) presents attractive opportunities for businesses seeking flexibility and innovation without logistical hurdles.

  Moreover, open-source communities contribute to

knowledge-sharing and collaboration, demystifying the processes required to create and deploy digital twins. An era emerges where collective expertise becomes a catalyst driving mainstream adoption—where seeking solutions transforms into finding synergy.

- **Education and Workforce Transformation**

  The digital imparting of skillsets is as imperative as technological enablers for a wide-scale transition. Educational institutions worldwide have incorporated digital twin concepts into curricula, ensuring that the emerging workforce possesses the expertise required to wield these technologies effectively.

  Universities and technical schools offer courses dedicated to digital twin applications, melding theoretical knowledge with practical skill development. Students engage in projects involving digital twins, equipping them with the proficiency to tackle challenges faced in real-world scenarios.

  Additionally, workforce transformation initiatives empower existing employees through training programs that bridge skills gaps, fostering a culture of digital competence. With empowered practitioners at its helm, the transition to mainstream digital twin use becomes a multifaceted collaboration of innovation and human capacity.

- **Standardization and Best Practices**

  As digital twins transition into mainstream use, industry leaders and thought leaders gravitate toward establishing standardized practices and frameworks. These initiatives aim to ensure

quality, consistency, and interoperability across
digital twin applications, solidifying their position
as trusted assets within technological landscapes.

Organizations such as the Industrial Internet
Consortium and ISO establish guidelines
shaping digital twin development, usage, and
application across global industries, offering
clarity and assurance to adopters navigating this
evolving field.   By cultivating a foundation of
standardization, industries enhance collaboration
and innovation, fostering an ecosystem where
digital twins thrive.

- **Challenges and Opportunities on the Pathway to
  Ubiquity**

Transitioning digital twins from niche applications
to mainstream integration is not without
challenges.   Barriers exist in the form of data
privacy concerns, integration complexities, and
management issues. However, these hurdles act
as foci for progress and collaboration, prompting
innovations in data governance, security, and
digital infrastructure.

As organizations tackle these challenges, they
unlock opportunities for renewed growth,
adept at maneuvering through complexities
and architecting cohesive solutions. The transition
to mainstream use becomes a dynamic narrative—
one underscored by adaptation, resilience, and
continuous evolution.

- **A Future Shaped by Digital Twins**

As digital twins become woven into the fabric
of modern industry, they transcend being
merely technology—they become catalysts of

44

transformation. This transition reflects broader societal changes in how we interact with, interpret, and influence the world. As ecosystems embody digital reflections of our reality, industries march toward a future rooted in understanding and insight—guided by a remarkable integration of the physical and digital.

Digital twins enrich decision-making, optimize resource allocation, and foster sustainability, forming a tapestry that defines industries of tomorrow. Their mainstream adoption symbolizes a retinal shift in progress, where data becomes a revered companion, shaping human endeavors and bridging the tangible with the virtual.

As we navigate this terrain, the transition to mainstream use reveals itself not as an end, but a beginning. A beginning where digital twins inspire, engage, and equip humanity with powerful perspectives—proving that, with insight and innovation, we can indeed shape the world in ways limited only by imagination.

In this journey, digital twins serve as navigators, guiding us through uncharted territories toward a potential laid not just in technology's embrace but in its inspiring endurance—and, like all great transitions, poised to leave an indelible mark on the world.

Chapter 3

How Digital Twins Work

Digital twins function by creating a digital replica of a physical entity through the integration of sensor data and analytical models. This seamless data flow enables real-time simulation and predictive analysis, which are crucial for optimizing operations and anticipating system failures. The interaction involves continuous feedback loops that refine system performance and support autonomous management features. This chapter delves into the underlying mechanisms of digital twins, illustrating their capability to enhance understanding and efficiency through sophisticated technology and data integration.

3.1   The Digital Replication Process

Imagine peering through a looking glass, not into another world, but into a digital version of our own—a version so detailed and dynamically connected to reality that it mirrors every heartbeat of its physical counterpart. This is the digital replication process, the origin point for every digital twin that extends the authority of the tangible into the boundless possibilities of the digital.

Cracking the Code of Reality

The concept of digital replication is rooted in an

47

age-old human desire to understand and control the environment. Replication, in essence, involves capturing the essence of the physical world and translating it into a digital canvas that can be observed, dissected, and manipulated. Imagine taking the molecular complexity of a cell and recreating it with pixels—this is the essence of the digital twin.

To achieve this, the process relies on an arsenal of sensors—the sentinels of modern technology. These sensors are the unsung heroes in industrial complexes, vehicles, city grids, and even personal devices. Like the fingertips of a master craftsman feeling the texture of material, sensors detect and capture data, providing the raw material from which digital twins are formed.

A Symphony of Data

The data harnessed by sensors encompasses myriad forms. From temperature and pressure to velocity and vibration, this treasure trove of information streams continuously from physical entities. Sensors regulate this constant flow, collecting, collating, and transmitting data that form tangible threads within the digital fabric.

Consider the example of wind turbines spread across a windswept landscape. Embedded sensors measure wind speed, blade rotation, mechanical strain, and atmospheric conditions—multisensory inputs that capture the dynamic interaction between environmental forces and structural response. This data becomes the lifeblood of the digital twin, weaving a tapestry of real-time insight and historical context.

Transmuting Physical Dynamics into Digital Reality

The transformation from the physical to the digital involves more than technical finesse; it requires conceptual clarity. This process calls upon advanced analytical models—mathematical blueprints—to interpret raw data, codifying them into a coherent digital form resembling its physical precursor.

Think of these models as translators capable of converting the complex dialect of reality into the precise language of code. They take raw data points and render them into three-dimensional constructs—a digital facsimile replete with dimensional accuracy, functional behavior, and interactional predictability. These constructs allow users to see beyond the real, delving into functions and processes unfettered by physical limitations.

A shining beacon of digital replication is found within the automotive industry. Consider a car operating within a city's latticework of roads, equipped with sensors that capture vehicular speed, engine performance, and traffic patterns. A digital twin of this vehicle encompasses these dynamic variables, enabling engineers to simulate various driving conditions and anticipate maintenance needs amid ever-changing terrains—a testament to the digital twin's capacity for real-time mirroring.

Digital Twin Incubation

The journey from data to digital twin involves an incubation-like phase, one that nurtures the nascent twin through cycles of model refinement and performance verification. Here, the digital twin must prove its fidelity—the extent to which it can encapsulate the nuances of its physical counterpart.

Verification rituals ensure that the digital twin echoes the dynamics of its physical originator. Stress tests, environmental simulations, and operational heuristics validate its performance and predictive accuracy. These trials act as a crucible, refining the twin as it learns to replicate its physical sibling with increasing precision.

Imagine the challenges facing an aerospace company striving to recreate the subtleties of aircraft operation. Digital twin models subject the virtual aircraft to simulated atmospheric conditions, structural stressors, and complex flight patterns. Through this digital gauntlet, every rivet and circuit is tested, ensuring fidelity in form and function.

Contextual Interpretation: From Data to Insight

The magic of digital replication does not reside solely in data collection but in the ability to distill it into actionable insights. Through graphical interfaces, dashboards, and analytical overlays, digital twins present their insights in intuitive, digestible formats. These interfaces transform cryptic data into comprehensible intelligence that guides decision-making.

For instance, in the medical field, a digital twin of a patient's organ system acts as an interactive tool that communicates health fluctuations or responses to treatment. Surgeons interact with this virtual representation to visualize surgical interventions, enhancing their understanding of physiological variables that exist beneath the surface.

A Living Digital Organism

Unlike static replicas that dismiss change, digital twins embrace evolution. Once integrated within operational workflows, digital twins adapt, refine, and respond to ever-shifting conditions. This dynamic relationship fosters a living digital organism—one that matures and grows alongside its physical partner.

Imagine an urban traffic management digital twin constantly adjusting routes based on real-time inputs, including traffic congestion, accidents, and pedestrian flows. This adaptive capability transforms static modelling into a fluid process of simulation and response, breathing life into the digital form as it dynamically interacts with the rhythms of city life.

Synthesizing Past and Future

Finally, digital twins offer a vision of synthesis—a confluence of historical data and future potential. By reconciling past performance with emerging trends, they provide organizations with predictive foresight—a glimpse into what might be, enabling proactive rather than reactive management.

In the energy sector, digital twins of power plants store vast amounts of operational data, enabling simulations that preempt equipment wear or anticipate energy demands. By merging past performance with prospective scenarios, utilities achieve operational excellence and contribute to sustainability goals, steering energy flows with precision and purpose.

As we unravel the digital replication process, it becomes clear that the emergence of digital twins represents more than technological achievement—it hails a paradigm shift in interaction with the physical world. Through precision in replication, creativity in interpretation, and dynamism in evolution, digital twins forge a bond between reality and imagination, offering a frontier where opportunities abound, inviting us to explore and innovate, one byte at a time.

3.2 Data Collection and Integration

In the symphony of digital advancement, data is the music, and digital twins are the conductors, orchestrating harmony between the digital and physical realms. Central to this process is the art and science of data collection and integration, a foundational element that empowers digital twins to mirror and inform reality with incredible fidelity and foresight.

The Lifeblood of Data

Data is often likened to the lifeblood that courses through the veins of modern technology, instilling it with vitality and purpose. In the context of digital twins, data is not merely a static asset—it is a dynamic latent force, poised to reveal insights and drive decisions. The process begins with data collection, an endeavor that involves a network of sensors and devices that continually capture the multifaceted dimensions of the physical world.

Historically, data collection has evolved alongside technological advancements. Where once data was logged manually, today it is captured instantaneously, thanks to an array of sensors embedded within physical systems. From the tremors sensed by seismographs to the vital signs monitored by medical devices, each data point contributes to a comprehensive representation of reality.

Consider the automotive industry, where sensors embedded within vehicles gather data on speed, fuel efficiency, emissions, and driver behavior. These informational streams not only form the basis of vehicular digital twins but empower manufacturers and users with unprecedented levels of operational insight, optimizing everything from safety features to navigation systems.

The Collection Process: Precision Instruments at Work

The precision of data collection lies not only in the technology utilized but in the strategic placement and calibration of sensors. These sensors range from the simple to the sophisticated, depending on their purpose and environment. On factory floors, industrial sensors capture machine vibrations and acoustic signals to forecast maintenance needs. In smart buildings, sensors monitor temperature, airflow, and occupancy, optimizing environmental controls.

Take agriculture—a sector where gadgetry and growth meet. Here, sensors transformed traditional practices by capturing soil moisture, nutrient levels, and microclimatic conditions. Farmers now harness data to tailor interventions, ensuring that crops neither wilt under thirst nor drown in deluge—a modern-day illustration of how data breathes life into ancient practices.

Navigating the Data Deluge

The digital age brings a paradox: a deluge of data but where to swim? With exponential growth in data volume, the challenge lies not in gathering data but in filtering out noise, maintaining accuracy, and ensuring relevance. This is where integration becomes critical—a process less akin to plumbing and more like choreography, weaving disparate strands into a coherent whole.

Aviation provides a compelling lens through which we understand this complexity. Airplanes are akin to mobile data centers, with myriad sensors monitoring every facet of flight, from engine thrust to cabin pressure. Through integration, these streams coalesce into actionable insights, guiding pilots and ground control in navigation, diagnostics, and emergency response—ensuring that where the digital twin ventures, safety follows.

Integration: Crafting a Cohesive Picture

Integrating data to form a digital twin demands finesse, akin to an artist blending colors on a palette to achieve

53

a masterpiece. It involves alignment, context, and oftentimes transformation, where raw data must be processed, cleaned, and structured to reveal its richness.

In healthcare, patient records, diagnostic images, and wearable device data converge to form personal digital twins. Here, integration translates to lifesaving outcomes, as doctors visualize a patient's condition in a holistic fashion. Surgery simulations and treatment protocols become tailored efforts, ensuring interventions that are bespoke rather than binary.

Confronting Challenges: Interoperability and Security

The path to seamless data integration is not without its obstacles. Chief among them is interoperability—the capacity for disparate systems to communicate harmoniously. With assorted data types flowing from diverse sources, standardization becomes paramount. Efficient integration demands common frameworks, as data must speak a unified language, free of translational errors.

Moreover, data security and privacy weigh heavily. With deeper insights comes the responsibility to shield sensitive information, ensuring that its use respects privacy and abides by ethical standards. Encryption, access controls, and audit trails become allies in a landscape where data's delicate dance must remain untarnished.

From Data to Action: The Feedback Loop

Once data is vogued and varnished through integration, it navigates the lifecycle of a digital twin, informing simulation models and predictive analytics. The feedback loop—a core feature of digital twins—relies on precise data integration to function, transforming raw input into insightful output.

Consider the logistics sector, where digital twins orchestrate supply chains with the precision of a Swiss watch. Real-time tracking data predicts delays and reroutes shipments preemptively, safeguarding supply commitments. By monitoring variables such as weather patterns and traffic, integrated data ensures logistics that remain steadfast amid uncertainty.

The Future: Beyond Collection and Integration

As digital twins proliferate, and as technology advances, data collection and integration will continue to evolve, heralding a future of increased granularity and interconnectivity. With 5G networks promising unprecedented speeds and edge computing reducing latency, real-time data integration will become ever more powerful and responsive.

In this unfolding narrative, data collection and integration transcend being enablers—they become architects of possibilities. By building interconnected webs of information, digital twins empower us to not only predict but to shape a future where systems interact intelligently, in a world more interconnected and insightful than ever before.

Thus, data collection and integration reveal themselves not merely as technological processes, but as dynamic conduits through which we glimpse and influence the tapestry of the modern world. A stage upon which digital twins engage, enlighten, and evolve, offering not just a mirror to reality but a compass to its future. Through the lens of data, digital twins unlock a realm of innovation, where the map of possibilities extends as far as imagination dares to venture.

3.3 Simulation and Analysis Mechanisms

In the theater of digital twins, simulation and analysis serve as the spotlight and script, breathing life and purpose into otherwise inert data streams. This section unravels the intricate mechanisms that empower digital twins to transcend mere replication, enabling them to predict futures, avert crises, and optimize performance all while inhabiting virtual spaces where creativity meets calculation.

A Glance Back: The Evolutionary Arc

To appreciate the sophistication of simulation and analysis in digital twins, it is helpful to look back at their lineage. Early computational simulations appeared in the mid-20th century, famously used by meteorologists harnessing primitive computer models to predict weather patterns, a domain historically resistant to human foresight.

Fast forward to the dawn of the space age, where NASA utilized early simulation tools to model spacecraft systems—a crucial step towards modern digital twins. These initial adaptations were foundational, allowing today's simulations to portray complexities once unimaginable—even down to the subatomic dance of particles within a material matrix.

As computing power surged, the computational ability to simulate intricate systems with precision became a widespread reality, laying the groundwork for the detailed analysis capabilities seen today in digital twins spanning diverse industries.

Simulation: The Virtual Voyage

Imagine, if you will, a vessel setting sail on uncharted

waters. Simulation acts as the ship's compass, mapping potential routes, testing conditions before they are faced in reality. In this digital realm, variables are not seen as confounding factors but as opportunities—altered, controlled, analyzed ad infinitum.

Take the automotive sector's approach to crash testing. Gone are the days when safety improvements relied solely on physical tests, each requiring cumbersome setups and, unfortunately, the sacrifice of vehicles. Now, digital twins simulate crashes repeatedly, subjecting virtual cars to a multitude of impact scenarios, adjusting parameters, and refining designs with a few clicks.

The result? Vehicles designed with enhanced safety features and shorter development cycles, as simulations provide a proving ground unconstrained by physical limitations—a modern crucible where models reveal not only design flaws but opportunities for innovation.

Digital Laboratories: Experimentation Unlimited

Central to the impact of simulations in digital twins is their role as digital laboratories, where myriad scenarios can be tested without consequence. This is especially transformative in fields governed by variables beyond human control.

Consider the pharmaceutical industry, where simulations delve into cellular environments under a digital microscope. Virtual clinical trials allow researchers to explore drug interactions across a broad spectrum of biological profiles—safeguarding patient welfare and expediting discovery processes. This simulation-based approach reduces costs and risks, bringing therapies from lab to bedside faster than traditional methods allow.

In the world of architecture and construction,

simulations empower designers and engineers to navigate complex blueprints. Not only do they model structural integrity, but they anticipate the impact of environmental conditions, material fatigue, and even human occupancy patterns. These virtual rehearsals help architects design buildings infused with resilience and efficiency—sheltered from the seismic shocks of real-world trial and error.

Analysis: Bridging Insight and Action

If simulation is the compass guiding a digital twin's voyage, then analysis is the insight, probing beneath the surface to decode hidden signals and patterns unveiled in the process. Ultimately, robust analysis transforms raw simulation outputs into actionable strategies.

Machine Learning and AI algorithms are the unsung heroes in this transformation. Embedded within digital twins, they function as analytical engines—detecting patterns, uncovering anomalies, and forecasting trends with speed and precision.

For instance, energy utilities harness digital twins to analyze power grid behavior, using simulations to assess load dynamics, predict fluctuations, and optimize distribution. Here, advanced analytics help operators avert blackouts, manage demand, and improve sustainability, enabling energy resources to flow like water instead of wading through restrictive dams.

Furthermore, predictive maintenance relies on analysis mechanisms within digital twins. By interpreting data signatures induced by machinery wear and tear, analytics predict future failures, preventing costly downtime. In sectors as varied as aerospace and manufacturing, predictable precision becomes the linchpin of operations, fortifying systems against unforeseen disruptions.

The Human Element: Intuition through Simulation

While digital twins wield the power of sophisticated algorithms, the human element remains vital. Far from obsolete, human intuition and decision-making are synergistically enhanced through simulation-based insights.

Consider healthcare, where digital twins collaborate with clinicians. Patient-specific simulations forecast treatment paths, integrating clinical expertise to tailor unique patient journeys. This union extends human foresight, transforming prognosis into partnership, where data-driven insights empower but do not replace, allowing caregivers to explore and choose optimal pathways for patient recovery.

A Symphony of Systems: Integration and Interoperability

The true genius of simulation and analysis within digital twins lies in their ability to integrate with other systems, creating a symphony of interconnected solutions. Platforms that connect multiple digital twins afford a panoramic view across enterprise networks—cross-pollinating insights and delivering coordinated actions.

In smart cities, simulations integrate transport, energy, and environmental systems into cohesive urban management strategies. Through real-time data analysis, scenarios like emergency responses or infrastructure planning become fluid operations—resilient and anticipatory, unfurling with precision in urban narratives woven by digital twins' insightful predictions.

The Future: Unbounded Possibilities

As we look towards the horizon, simulation and analysis mechanisms within digital twins promise an era of exploration unencumbered by constraints. The intersection of edge computing, augmented reality, and AI fortifies these capabilities, empowering digital twins to adapt and accelerate outcomes with unprecedented speed.

Envision precision agriculture, where simulations guide each step from seed to harvest, adapting to weather patterns and soil conditions informed by real-time insights—fulfilling humanity's ambition to feed the world sustainably and innovatively.

As digital twins meld simulation with analysis, they reshape tomorrow's landscapes, offering a toolkit for exploration as vast as imagination. Within their reach lies a world reflective of possibilities—one where virtual horizons shepherd us towards a sustainable, insightful, and dynamically evolving future. Through their lens, digital twins inspire us to view the dance of data as a choreography of progress—a vibrant reminder that while reality may be confining, in the realm of simulation, the sky is truly the limit.

3.4 Feedback Loops and System Optimization

Imagine standing at the helm of a ship, navigating uncharted waters with keen reliance on the ship's compass, radar, and the constellative guidance of stars. In much the same way, digital twins pilot enterprises through the ever-evolving seas of data, steered by the power of feedback loops. Feedback loops are the keystone, closing the circle between action and reaction, prediction and adjustment. They transform digital twins from passive entities into dynamic guides capable of shepherding systems toward peak efficiency.

The Virtuous Cycle of Information

Feedback loops in digital twins echo a foundational principle observed throughout nature and technology—the cyclical return of information improves decisions and behavior, creating a virtuous cycle of continuous enhancement. In digital twins, these loops facilitate real-time communication between the virtual and physical realms. Through a continuous exchange of data, insights gleaned from computations inform actions that shape the physical entity, which in turn update the twin—a seamless cycle of adaption and optimization.

Consider the complex landscape of smart manufacturing, where feedback loops operate as the beating heart of digital twin functionality. In a factory, machinery embedded with sensors collects data on operational efficiency, wear-and-tear, and output quality. This information is processed by the digital twin, which analyzes performance metrics and recommends pliable interventions. Fine-tuned adjustments are then implemented automatically or by engineers, refining production processes and reducing inefficiencies—each cycle honing the system to sharper levels of precision.

A Historical Perspective: Nature's Blueprint

Feedback mechanisms are not a modern invention. They are nature's foundational design, elegantly exemplified by biological systems. The human body, for instance, employs feedback loops to maintain homeostasis. When body temperature rises, mechanisms trigger sweating to cool it down; when glucose levels spike, insulin is released to manage sugar uptake—continuous cycles maintain balance and promote survival.

This biological precedent influenced early technological advances, where mechanical regulators such as James Watt's centrifugal governor on steam engines embodied basic feedback mechanisms, automatically adjusting valve openings to maintain a consistent engine speed— an innovation that led to more efficient industrial processes.

Frameworks of Control: From Cybernetics to Modern Computing

The mid-20th century saw feedback loops unfolding their wings within the emerging field of cybernetics, a transdisciplinary framework that studied regulatory systems, their structures, constraints, and possibilities. Cybernetics' exploration of self-regulation and communication within machines and organisms laid crucial theoretical foundations for modern feedback loops.

Today's digital twins, supported by advancements in AI and IoT, create sophisticated control systems where feedback mechanisms are indispensable tools. They facilitate adaptive learning, fostering a resilient and responsive digital twin environment where iterative improvement becomes not just possible, but fundamental.

Applications in Real-World Scenarios

Feedback loops have become indispensable across myriad sectors, where the harmony of precision and adaptiveness propels optimized operation.

- **Energy Management** Examine the energy sector, where digital twins leverage feedback loops to enhance power grid stability and efficiency. By continuously monitoring energy generation, distribution, and consumption, and integrating real-time data with predictive analytics, digital twins optimize grid loads, respond to fluctuations, mitigate wastage, and stabilize pricing—responsively adapting to both user demand and environmental inputs. Renewable energy sources, such as wind and solar, particularly benefit, as their inherently variable output demands precise modulation and storage strategies.

- **Building and Infrastructure** In architecture, feedback loops are elemental, enabling smart buildings to offer optimized living and working environments. HVAC systems continually collect data on occupancy, climate conditions, and energy usage; digital twins process this information, orchestrating heating, cooling, lighting, and ventilation to ensure comfort while conserving resources. This can significantly reduce energy costs and environmental footprints, while enhancing tenant satisfaction—a smart synergy between human need and machine optimization.

- **Healthcare** In healthcare, personalized medicine thrives through digital twins enhanced by patient-specific feedback loops. By monitoring real-time health data—such as heart rate, glucose levels, or respiratory function—digital twins simulate potential treatment outcomes and adjust interventions to maintain patient health. Consider diabetic patients, whose digital twins predict blood sugar fluctuations, adjusting insulin doses dynamically, offering focused treatment and averting complications before they manifest.

Challenges and Considerations

Despite the allure of feedback-driven optimization, challenges persist in implementing these mechanisms effectively. Real-time data processing demands robust computational capabilities and secure infrastructure—a necessity to ensure rapid data exchange and decision-making without compromising on accuracy or security.

Moreover, the deterministic nature of feedback loops must be complemented by human oversight— strategic thinking, creative problem-solving, and ethical considerations remain the purview of human intelligence. Balancing automation with human insight ensures systems evolve responsibly and meet the ethical standards of innovation.

The Future of Feedback Loops: Autonomous Horizons

As digital twin technology evolves, feedback loops will expand their role beyond reactive adjustments into realms of autonomy. Integration with machine learning and AI enables systems to not only respond to current data but anticipate future scenarios and shape pathways proactively—transforming digital twins from custodians to creators.

Autonomous vehicles illustrate this potential; digital twins governing their operations harness the combined force of feedback and predictive analytics, adapting routes based on traffic flow, environmental conditions, and individual driving behavior, promoting safety and efficiency.

Envision urban environments where citywide digital twins dynamically manage traffic signals, optimize public transit schedules, and adapt to changing urban landscapes. Here, feedback loops reconfigure city systems, fostering intelligent, more sustainable urban ecosystems.

A Closing Arc: Convergence and Continual Progress

Feedback loops in digital twins epitomize the convergence of digital and physical worlds, foreshadowing a future where adaptation and optimization become second nature—ceaseless, responsive, almost organic in locomotion. As systems grow more interconnected and intuitive, feedback loops nourish them, cultivating ecosystems that thrive on synergy and endless innovation.

While feedback loops are mechanisms grounded in rigorous exploration and craftsmanship, they enable a narrative filled with transformative potential. They teach us that in the digital era, progress is not a straight line but a circle, endlessly looping, each iteration bringing us closer to possibilities unchecked by previous constraints. Through optimization, digital twins not only map new territories of understanding—they invite us to reimagine our relationship with technology, and ask: what other frontiers might become visible as we listen to the echoes of feedback and follow their lead?

3.5 Collaborative and Autonomous Features

As technology advances, digital twins have emerged not just as tools for mirroring the physical world but as active participants in a digital ecosystem characterized by collaboration and autonomy. This evolution from passive replicas to dynamic entities capable of communication and self-governance signals a profound shift in how we engage with and utilize technology.

A Historical Perspective: The Road to Connectivity

The genesis of today's collaborative digital twins can be traced back to early networked systems in the late 20th century. As industries recognized the potential of interconnected devices, the groundwork was laid for systems that could share information. Early instances of rudi-

mentary collaboration can be seen in distributed computing and early forms of computer networking, where systems began to perform cooperatively, sharing workloads
and data across geographically diverse locations.

Fast forward to the modern era, and digital twins have
become powerful nodes within the expansive web of the
Internet of Things (IoT). Within this network, they transcend their original roles, acting not only as individual
replicas but as interconnected entities capable of seamless interaction and synchronized functioning.

Collaborative Capabilities: Symphony of Synchronicity

At the heart of a digital twin's collaborative potential
is its ability to connect, interact, and share information
with other systems, devices, and digital twins. This
interconnectedness leads to greater efficiency and
improved decision-making capabilities, heralding a
landscape where collaboration is the norm rather than
the exception.

- ## Healthcare: A Shared Vision of Wellness

  In healthcare, collaborative digital twins facilitate
  unprecedented levels of patient care through integrated data ecosystems. Imagine a network of digital twins representing individual patients, medical
  devices, and healthcare facilities all seamlessly in-
  teracting. This network allows doctors to gain real-
  time visibility into patient health, consult with specialists regardless of location, and even integrate
  predictive analytics to anticipate health issues.

  Digital twins take collaborative diagnostics to new
  heights, enabling personalized treatment plans
  crafted through collective insights—where each
  entity contributes to a holistic understanding of

patient health.

- **Supply Chains: Navigating the Nexus**

  In logistics, digital twins interconnect across supply chains, sharing critical data on inventory levels, transportation updates, and demand fluctuations. This real-time collaboration allows businesses to dynamically adjust manufacturing schedules, reroute shipments, and anticipate market changes.

  Picture a global consortium of manufacturers and suppliers using digital twins not only to optimize production but to predict potential disruptions caused by environmental conditions or geopolitical events. Collaborative features become a strategic advantage, ensuring continuity in even the most intricate supply webs.

- **Smart Cities: Integrated Urban Orchestration**

  Urban environments stand to benefit immensely from the collaborative capabilities of digital twins. By forming a networked digital twin ecosystem, cities can coordinate infrastructure, utilities, and services to improve quality of life for inhabitants.

  Comprehensive urban management involves digital twins representing transportation systems, utility grids, emergency services, and more, orchestrating a responsive cityscape that adapts to daily demands.

  Considered holistically, these collaborations extend beyond mere operational efficiency, nurturing urban ecosystems that are sustainable, resilient, and, most importantly, livable.

Autonomous Features: The Dawn of Independence

As digital twins gain collaborative prowess, their autonomous capabilities invite a transformational vista where self-sufficiency becomes increasingly achievable. Automation emerges as a defining attribute, enabling digital twins to independently perform tasks, make decisions, and adapt to changing environments without constant human intervention.

- **Manufacturing: Automated Ambitions**

  Within manufacturing plants, autonomous digital twins leverage real-time data to adjust production lines, allocate resources, and even respond to equipment malfunctions as they occur.

  Autonomous operations imbue manufacturing with unprecedented levels of adaptability, where digital twins detect inefficiencies, initiate corrective actions, and optimize workflows without human input—a hallmark of resilient and future-ready factories.

- **Agriculture: Smart Farms of Tomorrow**

  In agriculture, digital twins autonomously monitor and manage farm operations, collecting data from soil sensors, weather forecasts, and crop health indicators to dynamically tailor watering, fertilization, and pest control strategies.

  Through their autonomous capabilities, digital twins facilitate precision agriculture, ensuring optimal yields with minimal resource expenditure— heralding a future where smart farms operate in harmony with the land.

- **Transportation: Towards Driverless Horizons**

  Autonomous digital twins are pivotal players in the race toward driverless transportation. In conjunction with AI algorithms, they navigate routes, manage traffic flows, and respond to real-time road conditions, enhancing safety and efficiency in autonomous vehicles.

These autonomous capabilities extend beyond mere piloting; they encompass dynamic adaptation to environmental conditions, integrating diverse datasets to ensure seamless travel experiences where passengers become mere contemplators of landscapes rushing by.

The Human-Machine Interface: A New Balance

At the intersection of collaboration and autonomy lies a delicate balance between machine intelligence and human oversight. While digital twins navigate systems independently, human intuition remains indispensable, ensuring ethical considerations, creativity, and strategic thinking continue to guide machine actions.

Empowered by the collaborative and autonomous features of digital twins, human operators shift from practitioners to stewards—overseeing, guiding, and refining processes enhanced by digital acumen.

Challenges and Considerations

Despite the allure of a seamlessly connected and self-governing digital landscape, challenges accompany these advances. Interoperability remains a hurdle, as disparate systems evolve with varying standards, potentially hindering collaborative efforts. Effective collaboration requires a shared framework that reflects consistent data standards across interconnected digital twins.

Privacy and security pose additional considerations, where autonomous twins must be diligently monitored to protect sensitive data and ensure their actions align with ethical standards. As autonomy introduces complexity, it is crucial to navigate these challenges with diligence and care.

The Promise of a Collaborative and Autonomous Era

As we embrace the collaborative and autonomous features of digital twins, we unlock a future defined by integration and intelligence. The confluence of human creativity and digital prowess kindles a paradigm where technological evolution amplifies our potential, not merely automatons carrying out preordained scripts but vibrant, dynamic forces charting untraveled terrains.

This new chapter of digital twin evolution heralds a world resounding with potential and living systems, orchestrating symphonies of collaboration, adaptation, and autonomy where humanity's reach extends beyond the tangible into realms awash with innovation. Through the brilliant confluence of systems synchronized, we glimpse a horizon promising not just understanding but empowerment—a testament to unity, evolution, and boundless possibilities that await our collaborative embrace.

Chapter 4

Applications of Digital Twins Across Industries

Digital twin technology is revolutionizing a wide array of industries by providing enhanced process optimization and decision-making capabilities. In manufacturing, it streamlines production and reduces errors; in healthcare, it personalizes patient care and treatment planning. Urban planners and infrastructure developers use digital twins to create smarter cities, while the energy sector employs them for efficient resource management. The automotive and aerospace industries benefit through improved design, testing, and maintenance processes. This chapter explores these diverse applications, demonstrating how digital twins drive innovation and improve efficiency across sectors.

4.1   Manufacturing and Production

Imagine a factory floor, a buzzing hub of machinery and activity, where every cog, wheel, and lever works in symphonic precision to produce everything from smartphones to automobiles. Now, picture this dynamic landscape mirrored by its digital counterpart, each machine having a digital twin that not only replicates

71

its current state but also predicts future performance and potential issues. Welcome to the transformative realm where digital twin technology intersects with manufacturing and production.

The Age of Transformation

The industrial evolution, driven initially by steam and electricity, has now embraced the digital revolution as its new catalyst, propelling manufacturing into an era where digital twins are indispensable tools of innovation. Beyond analog renderings, these digital counterparts offer a multiverse of possibilities—optimizing processes, enhancing quality control, and ensuring peak synchronicity between human and machine.

Historically, manufacturing has been built on the principles of replication and efficiency. Henry Ford's assembly line revolutionized production by cutting costs while increasing output. Today, the tradition of efficiency is carried forth by digital twins, which infuse data-driven insights into operations, pushing the boundaries of what an assembly line can achieve.

Process Optimization: From Guesswork to Precision

In the bustling world of production, the gold standard has always been precision—delivering products that meet exact specifications without waste or delay. Digital twins revolutionize this endeavor by visualizing and analyzing the production process in real-time.

Consider the case of Siemens, a leader in leveraging digital twins within its manufacturing operations. At their state-of-the-art production facilities, each piece of machinery is mirrored by a digital twin that receives continuous data flows, analyzing performance metrics and suggesting optimal settings for speed, pressure, and temperature.

This real-time feedback loop empowers plant managers to make minute modifications to the fabrication process—turning the calibration knob here, adjusting a conveyor belt there. The result? A seamless confluence of technology and human acumen, ensuring efficiency and minimizing downtime caused by unforeseen hiccups.

In precision, digital twins usher a modern renaissance of tailor-made manufacturing—where machines anticipate variables and align efforts toward shared goals, creating products that consistently meet quality benchmarks.

Enhancing Quality Control

Creating a flawless product is the holy grail of manufacturing, but achieving perfection requires relentless vigilance. Digital twins play the role of tireless sentinels, monitoring every stage of production. By assimilating data into virtual models, these digital versions simulate wear and tear, predict failures, and even assess the impact of minute deviations.

Take General Electric (GE), for example, using digital twins to scrutinize their jet engine production lines. The digital replicas detect engine anomalies early, allowing the company to rectify issues before they materialize into costly defects. Digital twins thus safeguard the production pipeline, ensuring that every bolt fits perfectly, every turbine spins effortlessly, and every safety protocol is met with confidence.

Equipped with this proactive presence, factories no longer look backward at defects found too late; instead, they gaze forward, leveraging analytics to prevent errors and uphold product quality throughout supply chains.

Reducing Downtime: Keeping the Wheels Turning

Production downtime is manufacturing's arch-nemesis, turning factories into silent spaces while ticking up costs. But fortunately, digital twins act as oracles of foresight, predicting potential malfunctions before they disrupt workflow.

Consider the automotive industry, where every second of downtime can translate into significant financial losses. Digital twins in such settings offer real-time monitoring via interconnected sensor networks, predicting machine component degradation with high accuracy.

A car manufacturer, such as Toyota, can then use these insights to pre-schedule maintenance or replace parts during lull periods, ensuring that production lines never skip a beat. Efficiency is preserved, and the rhythm of progress never falters.

Case Study: A Digital Twin Success Story

One of the most illustrative applications of digital twins is Bosch's Factory of the Future initiative, where AI-driven digital twins enable adaptive manufacturing. Each manufacturing cell can autonomously adapt to produce new products as needs evolve, informed by the digital twin's analyses and predictions.

This adaptability means the factory can shift between tasks as demands fluctuate, with minimal human intervention. The digital twins make decisions based on holistic datasets, optimizing resource allocation and ensuring no parts or energy are squandered. Factories become ecosystems, where machines and data coexist harmoniously to achieve seamless outputs.

Pioneering Sustainable Production

As industries pivot towards sustainability, digital twins offer pathways not only for optimizing production but also minimizing environmental footprints. By simulating resource consumption and waste generation, digital twins guide manufacturers towards eco-friendly practices, such as energy-efficient operations or material salvage.

Imagine a clothing manufacturer using digital twins to track fabric usage during garment construction. By reducing excess fabric waste, they not only cut costs but also promote sustainable production cycles. This duality of profit and planet aligns with corporate social responsibility aspirations, pushing factories toward greener futures.

The Continued Evolution

As the narrative of manufacturing and production intertwines with digital twins, the potential for innovation seems boundless. The convergence of IoT, AI, and digital twins heralds an era of 'smart manufacturing', where adaptability and foresight are routine, and optimization is continuous.

Furthermore, as advances in machine learning unfold, digital twins will evolve into even more sophisticated allies—predictive engines analyzing vast data libraries to craft dynamic production strategies based on market trends, material availability, or consumer preferences.

Looking Ahead

In sum, digital twins are not mere mirrors reflecting reality; they are dynamic partners steering manufacturing into an era of unparalleled precision and potential. They elevate factories into digital phenomena, where processes echo efficiency and outputs seek perfection.

Through the lens of digital twins, the future of manufacturing is a panorama of progress—an amalgamation of art and science infusing every cog and wheel with the imagination that dared to transform yesterday's assembly lines into tomorrow's avant-garde production platforms. As more industries embrace this transformation, the stories of manufacturing's achievements will echo the promise and possibilities of an era where innovation knows no bounds—inviting us to dream, create, and refine along the journey to a bold, digitized frontier.

4.2   Healthcare and Medicine

Imagine a world where every heartbeat, every cellular anomaly, every nuanced response to medication can be visualized, analyzed, and optimized through the lens of a digital twin. In the complex tapestry of healthcare and medicine, digital twins are weaving threads of possibility that transform how we approach patient care, treatment customization, and system efficiency.

From Historical Roots to Digital Realities

While the idea of a digital twin may seem futuristic, its essence is deeply rooted in the age-old human aspiration to understand and heal the body through replication and simulation. Throughout history, the medical field has strived for precision—from the anatomical sketches of Leonardo da Vinci, tracing the intricate mechanics of the human body, to the first X-rays allowing glimpses into our hidden anatomical world.

Just as X-rays revolutionized understanding, digital twins promise a similar leap, elevating medicine from reactive care to predictive precision. The journey now fuses data science with biomedicine, painting a digital portrait of human physiology and pathology, offering insights akin to holding a diagnostic crystal ball.

The Personal Health Odyssey: Patient-Specific Digital Twins

In this era of personalized medicine, digital twins are the harbingers of individualized healthcare, crafting patient-specific simulations that consider genetic, environmental, and lifestyle factors. Each patient becomes a unique narrative, with their digital doppelgänger translating nuanced health data into actionable insights.

Consider the realm of cardiology. With cardiovascular disease claiming lives across the globe, digital twins offer cardiologists invaluable simulation tools. A digital twin of a patient's heart—constructed from imaging technologies and real-time sensor data—can simulate blood flow, predict arrhythmias, and even model the impact of surgical interventions or medication regimes.

This capability transforms care from one-size-fits-all to bespoke strategies, allowing for pre-emptive interventions. Physicians see beyond mere symptoms, peering into the interconnected dance of physiology and treatment optimization—a journey towards healing defined by precision.

Revolutionizing Diagnostics: Seeing Beyond the Surface

Digital twins have equally transformative potential in diagnostics, where speed and accuracy are vital. Take oncology, where early detection can make the difference between life and death. Digital twins model tumor evolution, simulating various growth scenarios and responses to treatment.

Imagine a cancer patient whose digital twin evaluates genetic mutations and predicts drug efficacy—transforming chemotherapy from a trial-and-error approach to a targeted therapeutic journey. This level of insight fosters informed decision-making, ensuring treatment paths are chosen with both hope and evidence at their cores.

Streamlined Clinical Trials and Drug Development

The pharmaceutical industry, fraught with lengthy clinical trials and soaring R&D costs, has embraced digital twins as a solution to expedite the drug development process. Virtual trials simulate patient interactions with drugs, predicting efficacy and identifying side effects before human trials commence.

Pharmaceutical giants such as AstraZeneca employ virtual pharmacokinetic models to understand how new compounds interact within the body.   These simulations sift through vast molecular libraries, optimizing candidate selection, potentially saving billions in development costs while increasing the speed at which potential cures reach those in need.

Hospital Efficiency: The Smart Healthcare System

Beyond individual care, digital twins optimize entire healthcare systems. Hospitals, intertwined with data ecosystems, harness digital simulations to streamline operations, manage resources, and enhance patient safety—each hospital room an orchestrated hub of efficiency.

Consider emergency departments, where patient flows are predicted and orchestrated by digital twin simulations. These assist in resource allocation—predicting patient loads based on historical data, seasonal trends, and even local events—ensuring staff, equipment, and space are utilized optimally to reduce wait times and improve care outcomes.

Pandemic Preparedness and Response

The COVID-19 pandemic cast a glaring spotlight on the need for advanced preparation and response mechanisms.   Digital twins have become pivotal in modeling virus spread and evaluating containment strategies, serving as virtual testbeds for policy response.

Countries employ digital twins to simulate the impact of interventions, such as social distancing or vaccination campaigns, assessing their effectiveness in real-time pandemics. These models support public health officials in formulating evidenced-based strategies, ensuring that responses strike a balance between public safety and societal functioning.

Patient Empowerment and Engagement

One of the most exciting prospects of digital twins in healthcare is the empowerment of patients. As wearables and health apps proliferate, individuals gain agency over their health data. Their digital twins offer insights into lifestyle impacts, treatment efficacy, and wellness journeys—fueling informed discussions with healthcare providers.

Consider a diabetes patient who uses continuous glucose monitoring, interfaced with a digital twin to gauge dietary impacts and medication effects. Informed with real-time feedback, they craft personalized lifestyle adjustments, championing autonomy through technology's supportive embrace.

Ethical and Privacy Considerations

With great potential, however, come ethical responsibilities. Patient data is a powerful resource, prompting digital twin architecture to prioritize security, privacy, and informed consent. Establishing standards and safeguarding information against malicious threats is vital, ensuring that digital twins serve as custodians of trust in the healthcare continuum.

Looking Forward: A New Horizon for Healing

The journey of digital twins in healthcare—from

concepts grounded in centuries past to the avant-
garde of modern medical practice—illustrates their
transformative potential in bridging gaps between
human biology and health technology. As the industry
continues to evolve, digital twins will guide us into an
era defined by precision, prevention, and personalized
care.

Their capacity to unify disparate datasets into coherent
medical narratives holds promise for a new standard in
healthcare—where cures are as unique as the patients
they benefit and where the convergence of technology
and compassion charts a definitive path to improved outcomes.

Thus, through digital twins, healthcare is not merely
improved; it is reimagined as a landscape of potential,
where each patient stands at the forefront of their own
story—a story informed by intelligence, guided by
empathy, and empowered by innovation. As these
digital reflections grow richer in data and capability,
they illuminate a future where the art and science
of medicine intertwine to craft pathways to better
health, beckoning us forward with each transformative
advance, sparking life in digital depth and opening
vistas of healing and hope.

4.3 Urban Planning and Infrastruc-
ture

The hum of a city is a complex symphony of interwoven
elements—housing, transport, utilities, and green
spaces, all coexisting like the intricate parts of a
massive, living organism. Effective urban planning
and infrastructure development are essential to keep
this urban organism thriving, and digital twins offer

a transformative tool to enhance these efforts. They provide a digital replica of urban environments, allowing planners to visualize, analyze, and refine urban spaces, thereby transforming the abstract dream of smart cities into tangible reality.

From Blueprints to Bytes: A Historical Perspective

Urban planning traces its roots back to ancient civilizations. Cities like Mohenjo-Daro and Rome exhibited early forms of systematic planning with grid layouts and aqueducts. These were physical representations of visionary ideas. Fast forward to the modern age, and the drafting table is replaced with digital landscapes. Here, digital twins shine—turning blueprints into bytes, crafting virtual city models that guide development with unprecedented precision.

This evolution has been driven by the need for sustainable expansion, efficient resource use, and enhanced quality of life. As cities grow and swell with human activity, traditional planning methods struggle to predict their dynamic behavior. Enter digital twins, carrying the promise of integration, innovation, and insight.

Crafting Dynamic Urban Models

Creating a digital twin for a city involves integrating vast layers of data—from geographical and environmental information to demographics and traffic patterns. The result is a living digital organism that reflects every facet of city life, allowing planners to visualize interactions and anticipate future needs.

This transformation is akin to a conductor assembling an orchestra: each dataset becomes an instrument, contributing vital information and perspective. When united, these elements produce harmonies that guide urban planning strategies within a city's characteristic tempo.

Take Singapore as a case study. Known globally for its commitment to smart city principles, Singapore employs digital twins of its urban landscape to manage infrastructure and resources. Transport systems, energy grids, and housing developments are coordinated through these virtual models to ensure optimal function and sustainability.

Enhanced Decision-Making and Scenario Analysis

Digital twins empower urban planners with the ability not only to visualize existing conditions but also to test potential development scenarios. This capability shifts the paradigm from reactive adjustment to proactive planning—a welcome evolution in an era where cities must adapt rapidly to changing demands and disruptions.

Consider a city grappling with traffic congestion. Planners can simulate the effects of constructing a new transit line or altering road layouts in a digital twin, analyzing potential outcomes on traffic flow, pollution levels, and commute times before making costly physical investments. These simulations present a safe environment in which to explore imaginative solutions and evaluate their impacts empirically.

Furthermore, digital twins facilitate resource allocation by incorporating data such as water consumption patterns or energy usage. This allows for a targeted approach to infrastructure upgrades, ensuring that resources are invested where they will have the greatest impact and benefit.   For instance, simulations in Melbourne are guiding water management strategies, ensuring that the city remains resilient in the face of climate variability.

Disaster Preparedness and Resilience

As climate change exacerbates the frequency and intensity of natural disasters, cities require robust strategies for resilience. Digital twins play a crucial role in disaster preparation and response by simulating various scenarios, conforming to pathways of mitigation and recovery.

Take flood-prone Amsterdam, where digital twins model the city's extensive canal and dyke systems. By simulating potential heavy rainfall events, planners can assess flood risks and optimize emergency response plans, ensuring that the city remains safe and its infrastructure resilient.

Moreover, real-time data feeds into digital twins during actual events, offering critical insights into evolving conditions and aiding in decision-making when time is of essence. A digital twin's ability to adapt on-the-fly enhances our capacity to safeguard urban environments from unpredictable threats.

Innovative Urban Experiences

Digital twins enable the creation of truly smart cities by fostering innovative urban experiences that prioritize citizens' well-being. These experiences arise through seamlessly integrating technology, enhancing accessibility, safety, and the quality of public services.

An example can be found in Stockholm, where digital twins are utilized to optimize public transportation networks. Commuters receive real-time service information that dynamically adjusts based on conditions such as traffic congestion or inclement weather, making travel planning as stress-free as possible, and ensuring efficiency in urban mobility.

These innovations extend beyond transport. Enhanced urban experiences include ensuring public parks and recreational facilities are equitably distributed, monitored, and managed. By aligning digital strategies with community needs, cities can invigorate public spaces into vibrant centers of engagement.

Fostering Public Engagement

A profound benefit of digital twins in urban planning lies in their ability to foster public engagement. Planners can employ visual simulations to communicate intended projects to city stakeholders, ensuring that citizens remain informed and engaged throughout the decision-making process.

Consider a proposal to develop a downtown area. By utilizing digital twins, planners can offer interactive simulations, showcasing design aesthetics, infrastructure impacts, and environmental considerations. This accessibility demystifies planning processes, inviting constructive dialogue and community feedback, leading to projects that garner public support and address collective aspirations.

Ethical and Practical Considerations

In adopting digital twins, planners must navigate ethical and practical considerations, such as data privacy and equity. The collection and integration of urban data must be handled with care to ensure that personal information is protected and that digital resources empower all sectors of society inclusively.

The challenge lies in striking a balance—leveraging data-driven insights without compromising ethical standards or fostering inequality. As digital twins become more integral to urban planning, establishing clear governance frameworks will be essential to ensure their equitable and safe application.

Envisioning the Future

The promise of digital twins in urban planning and infrastructure is undeniable—the opportunity to create resilient, sustainable, and vibrant urban environments is at hand. As cities continue to evolve and expand, the adoption of this technology will inevitably shape the future of urban landscapes worldwide.

Through immersive digital simulations and analyses, planners can explore uncharted avenues, bringing the boldest urban visions to life and optimizing the connective tissue of a city's infrastructure—from roads and bridges to energy and water networks.

The emergence of digital twins heralds an era where urban environments are not just built but crafted—sculpted by insights grounded in an understanding of how cities breathe, interact, and evolve. By embracing the potential of digital twins, we embark on a journey toward urban spaces that resonate with innovation, empathy, and intelligence, ensuring that as we build, we build wisely, creating cities that are as dynamic and adaptable as the populations they serve.

4.4 Energy and Utilities

In the expansive sphere of energy and utilities, where the quest for sustainability, efficiency, and reliability is perpetual, digital twins emerge as transformative agents of change. By digitally replicating complex systems, they offer unparalleled insights into how energy is produced, distributed, and consumed—allowing us to meet the demands of a growing population while mitigating the impact on our planet.

From Smoke to Simulations: A Historical Emergence

The story of energy begins with coal-stoked furnaces powering the Industrial Revolution, evolving through the electrification era and into the digital age. As energy infrastructure expanded, the need for innovative management and optimization became apparent, laying the groundwork for digital twin integration.

These technological advancements have precipitated a shift from reactive to predictive approaches in energy management, transforming how utilities operate and interact with the environment and consumers. Digital twins represent a distilled essence of this shift, wielding the power of real-time data and predictive analytics to drive informed decision-making.

Generating Insights: The Power of Digital Twins in Energy

Central to energy management is the production phase, where digital twins enhance the efficiency and resilience of generation assets. By providing a virtual model of power plants, turbines, and other generation equipment, digital twins allow operators to monitor performance, identify anomalies, and optimize maintenance schedules.

Consider wind farms, vast landscapes dotted with aerodynamic warriors harnessing the breeze. Digital twins replicate each turbine, analyzing metrics like blade pitch, wind direction, and rotor speed. These insights allow operators to optimize turbine performance and predict failure points, resulting in increased energy capture and reduced operational costs.

Similarly, in thermal power plants, digital twins simulate combustion processes, thermal cycles, and emission levels. This assists in minimizing fuel consumption and reducing environmental impact while maintaining optimal energy output—a fine-tuned balance between economy and ecology.

The Grid: A Digital Tapestry of Integration

Beyond generation, the electricity grid poses its own set of challenges—a complex web of transmission and distribution lines, substations, and transformers. Historically, managing this network involved reactive and often inefficient strategies, but digital twins have rewritten the rule book.

Grid operators now use digital twins to model entire electrical networks, forecasting load demand, pinpointing vulnerabilities, and testing the impact of new technologies like renewable energy sources or electric vehicles. By simulating extreme weather events or equipment failures, digital twins enable utility companies to devise contingency plans and minimize outage durations.

One illustrative example lies in Southern California Edison's use of digital twins to manage its vast grid. Through real-time simulations and data analytics, they optimize power flows, accommodate fluctuating renewable inputs, and ensure reliable service across the region, all while reducing costs and enhancing grid resilience.

Promoting Efficiency: The Promise of Smart Utilities

Smart grids and smart meters symbolize the intersection of consumer interaction and energy efficiency. Digital twins elevate this interaction by enabling a two-way flow of information between utilities and customers, fostering real-time communication and promoting energy conservation.

In urban environments, digital twins monitor electricity consumption patterns through smart meters, providing utilities with actionable insights to optimize load management and minimize peak demand. Meanwhile, consumers receive feedback on usage habits, empowering them to make more informed choices about energy consumption.

Example cities such as Copenhagen champion this approach, blending digital twin technology with public sustainability initiatives to reduce carbon footprints and promote clean energy use. The seamless integration of digital twins ensures that every kilowatt-hour is scrutinized, rationalized, and effectively utilized.

Renewable Revolution: Navigating New Frontiers

As nations worldwide commit to transitioning from fossil fuels to renewable energy sources, digital twins serve as indispensable navigational tools on this transformative journey. They facilitate the integration of solar, wind, and hydropower into existing energy systems, ensuring reliable delivery even amidst weather variances and natural fluctuations.

Take solar energy, where photovoltaic arrays stand at the forefront of renewable power generation. Digital twins model solar farms, analyzing variables like sun exposure, panel efficiency, and module temperature. This modeling allows operators to adapt reconfigurations autonomously, capitalizing on peak productivity and minimizing shading losses.

In hydroelectric power, digital twins simulate water flow dynamics and turbine interactions, providing predictive maintenance schedules and optimizing river management policies. Operators can thus plan around seasonal changes or drought conditions, securing stable energy supplies throughout the year.

Ensuring Reliability: Proactive Maintenance and Risk Management

Maintenance forms the backbone of reliability in energy

and utility sectors—a prerequisite often challenged by complex infrastructure and unpredictably harsh environments. Digital twins address this issue head-on, equipping operators with anticipatory capabilities that preemptively counter potential disruptions.

Through continuous monitoring, digital twins detect early signs of equipment degradation—temperature variations, vibration anomalies, or pressure fluctuations. Operators then receive predictive alerts, enabling them to schedule interventions before minor faults escalate into catastrophic failures.

An example in practice can be seen in the operations of Vattenfall, a prominent European energy company. By employing digital twins in their maintenance strategy, they have significantly reduced downtime and maintenance costs, enhancing overall service reliability and extending asset lifespans.

Beyond Energy: Scenarios to Shape the Future

Imagine a future where digital twins drive innovation beyond mere energy management—into applied research, policy development, and educational tools fostering sustainable thinking. By simulating new energy solutions or modeling consumer behavior, they inspire strategies capable of fostering innovation and reducing barriers to renewable adoption.

Additionally, digital twins could inform policy decisions by modeling the long-term impacts of regulatory changes or energy subsidies. Policymakers could leverage these insights to develop more effective electricity markets, encouraging sustainable development while ensuring fair and equitable access to resources.

Challenges Yet Opportunities

As digital twins scale across energy and utilities, challenges accompany their deployment—chief among them the need for data integrity, cybersecurity, and interoperability.   Reliable and secure data sharing is paramount to ensure confidentiality and trust in interconnected ecosystems.

However, these challenges present opportunities for collaborative problem-solving, inspiring cross-sector efforts to establish data standards, enhance cyber protections, and integrate legacy systems.   By overcoming these hurdles, digital twins will unlock the full potential of digital energy management.

The Way Forward: A Sustainable Horizon

Through digital twins, the energy industry stands poised at a historic crossroads—one where tradition meets transformation, and sustainability becomes a shared commitment rather than an individual aspiration.

Embracing these tools promises to refine energy processes, realizing efficiencies that transcend traditional limitations and forging a sustainable, resilient landscape.   As digital twins weave their way into the fabric of energy and utilities, they unveil a vibrant tapestry of possibility—one where innovation dances boldly in shadows cast by climate change and resource scarcity.

Guided by digital twins, we step towards a horizon that beckons with the promise of smarter energy—a future where our demands are met with prudence, our innovations are wrought with resilience, and our ecosystems flourish anew, refreshed by insight and inspired by the limitless potential that technology provides.

4.5 Automotive and Aerospace

Envision the automotive and aerospace sectors as twin titans of innovation, their vast complexities navigated with precision and artistry. Crucially, in recent years, digital twins have emerged as essential co-pilots, driving advancements across design, testing, and maintenance phases—essentially redefining what it means to take to the roads and skies.

Grounded in Tradition: Historical Context and Technological Evolution

Both the automotive and aerospace industries have storied histories that evoke images of mechanical marvels and groundbreaking aerodynamics. The automotive industry revved to life in the late 19th century, steering humanity into a new era of mobility with horseless carriages. Parallelly, aerospace found its wings with the Wright brothers' inaugural powered flight in 1903, accelerating our quest to conquer the skies.

However, these industries did not remain static. They evolved relentlessly alongside technological progress—from Ford's assembly line revolution that democratized car ownership to the turbojet engines that opened the era of supersonic flight. Yet, it is the fusion of digital transformation that now sets the stage for a radical reimagining, facilitated by digital twins.

Streamlining Design: From Concept to Creation

In the creative crucible of design, digital twins emerge as indispensable allies. Gone are the days of relying solely on physical prototypes; now, intricate simulations allow engineers to explore and iterate designs in a virtual landscape long before a model takes physical form.

In the automotive world, giants like Tesla employ digi-

tal twins in designing electric vehicles, simulating every
component from battery performance to aerodynamics.
This digital sandbox not only accelerates design cycles
but mitigates risk by identifying flaws or inefficiencies
before prototypes roll off production lines.

Similarly, airplane manufacturers such as Boeing leverage digital twins to model aircraft designs with unerring
precision. Simulations assess structural stability, aerodynamic performance, and passenger comfort, enabling
engineers to visualize the skies before the first test flight.
This approach optimizes aircraft design, reducing development time and cost while enhancing safety and performance.

The Rigors of Testing: Simulate, Iterate, Validate

For both cars and aircraft, rigorous testing is indispensable. Digital twins transform this landscape by
supplementing—and in some cases, supplanting—
traditional methodologies with data-rich simulations.

Consider crash testing, a staple in automotive safety verification. Instead of destructive and costly physical tests,
digital twins simulate crashes hundreds of times, variables altered with each iteration. These virtual impacts
inform design tweaks that enhance occupant safety, enabling engineers to make well-founded improvements
derived from the depth of computational analysis.

In aerospace, the challenge of testing aircraft components under extreme conditions is similarly daunting.
Enter digital twins, which replicate environmental
stresses; they accelerate the validation of materials
under various thermal, pressure, and vibrational forces.
Through these simulations, maintenance schedules
and potential failure points are elucidated, ensuring
component reliability before actual flights take place.

Beyond Manufacturing: Operational Efficiency and Predictive Maintenance

Once vehicles and aircraft are operational, digital twins extend their utility into the realms of efficiency and maintenance. By continuously monitoring performance in real-time, digital twins detect emerging anomalies and predict maintenance needs, preventing costly unscheduled downtime.

In the automotive sector, digital twins of connected cars analyze engine health, fuel consumption, and tire conditions, alerting drivers to potential issues before they become critical. For fleet managers, this predictive capability translates into optimized operations, where vehicle downtime is minimized and fleet efficiency maximized.

Aerospace also capitalizes on digital twin technology to augment operational ownership. Airlines leverage digital twins not just to monitor aircraft health but to anticipate maintenance or system checks. Aircraft components, from engines to landing gears, feed data to their digital counterparts, who crunch variables to predict wear and optimize servicing schedules. This foresight ensures aircraft spend more time cruising altitudes than resting on tarmacs.

The Road to Autonomy: Navigating the Future

Perhaps the most tantalizing horizon in both automotive and aerospace is the venture towards autonomy—a future where vehicles and aircraft operate with minimal human intervention.

In the automotive domain, autonomous vehicles harness digital twins to navigate through urban chaos, analyzing traffic patterns, pedestrian movements, and environmental conditions. By simulating these dynamic interactions, digital twins help refine those elusive smart algorithms piloting these driverless dervishes, transforming speculative sci-fi into pragmatic near reality.

Similarly, the aerospace industry eyes autonomous aircraft as a disruptive innovation. While fully autonomous airplanes may remain in the future, strides in unmanned aerial vehicles (UAVs) already demonstrate the potential for digitally enhanced navigation and control, aided by digital twins in ensuring safe and efficient operations.

Case Study Spotlight: Formula 1 Racing

Beyond commercial vehicles and aircraft, digital twins sprint ahead in the high-stakes world of Formula 1 racing, known for its relentless pursuit of technological edge.

Formula 1 teams integrate digital twins into their operational core, transforming racecar performance. These virtual race companions simulate aerodynamics, tire wear, and fuel consumption, providing live feedback during races. Strategists gain actionable insights, allowing split-second decisions on pit stops or adjustments to optimize race outcomes. In a world where milliseconds separate victory from defeat, digital twins are unrivalled co-pilots in the quest for podium glory.

Challenges on the Horizon: Navigating Complexity and Data Governance

While digital twins offer unparalleled possibilities, their integration involves addressing inherent challenges. The complexity of building robust digital models reflects the intricate interplay of systems in vehicles and aircraft.

Moreover, the relentless flow of data sparks concerns around managing cybersecurity and ensuring data governance. Protecting sensitive information from breaches, while ensuring transparency and accountability, is paramount to fostering trust and innovation within these industries.

As regulatory frameworks evolve, they must balance enabling technological possibilities while securing data-driven systems and protecting consumer privacy—a vigilant partnership between innovation and oversight.

The Intersection of Imagination and Reality

Digital twins are charting course towards an intersection where imagination and reality converge seamlessly. In doing so, they redefine the possibilities of design, testing, and operation, leading to advancements that elevate safety, efficiency, and innovation across automotive and aerospace domains.

These sectors, twin dynamos of industry advancement, find themselves empowered by digital twins to boldly dream and diligently pursue technologies that once whispered in the wings of ambition. They mark an epoch where our aspirational dreams of flight and freedom rev the engine of progress into a reality distinguished by insight, ingenuity, and foresight.

As digital twins continue to evolve, the road and sky become canvases mapped by precision, heralding a future where innovation knows no bounds—evidence that even as we grasp the wheel or soar on wings, the journey into the future is exhilaratingly open and expansive.

Chapter 5

Benefits and Challenges of Implementing Digital Twins

Digital twins provide numerous benefits, including enhanced operational efficiency, cost reduction, and improved decision-making through predictive insights. They offer scalability and adaptability across various applications, fostering innovation. However, implementing digital twins presents challenges such as complex technical requirements, data integration issues, and the need for significant investment in skills and resources. Addressing these challenges is essential for maximizing the technology's potential. This chapter examines both the advantages and hurdles associated with adopting digital twins, providing a balanced view of their impact on businesses and industries.

5.1 Operational Efficiency and Cost Reduction

In the quest for competitive advantage, businesses have always sought ways to refine processes, cut costs, and maximize efficiency. Enter digital twins, the digital replicas that supervise, simulate, and sometimes surpass the capabilities of their physical counterparts, heralding a new era of operational acumen. Through a confluence of real-time data and predictive analytics, digital twins illuminate pathways to efficiency that once lay obscured in complexity and conjecture.

A Brief Contemplation on Efficiency: From Steam Engines to Silicon

To appreciate the current revolution, we must acknowledge history's whispers of efficiency. From James Watt's improvements to the steam engine that powered the Industrial Revolution to Henry Ford's assembly line, each innovation thrived on the principle of doing more with less—less time, less waste, less effort. These ideas have, over centuries, somersaulted into the digital age where the infinite dexterity of digital twins promises levels of efficiency previously embodied only by the sleekest machines of fantasy.

In the past, predicting when a machine might falter was part science, part guesswork. Maintenance was scheduled on regular intervals, cruder inspections, and, at times, blind intuition. Today, digital twins revoke the need to guess. Machines may still wear and tear, but digital twins, equipped with sensor-fed streams of consciousness, transform opaque processes into transparent, manageable systems.

Real-Time Monitoring and Predictive Power

One of the seminal capabilities of digital twins lies in their relentless provision of real-time monitoring. Armed with streams of data from sensors embedded in equipment and facilities, these digital replicas provide a constant, live stream of information about operational conditions. This capability provides businesses with a panoramic view into the complexities of their processes.

Consider a manufacturing plant, where the orchestrated dance of machinery and manpower can be suddenly interrupted by a debilitated conveyor or ailing assembly unit. Normally, detecting the symptoms might take time, but digital twins can flag anomalies with alacrity, drawing attention to subtle vibrations or temperature changes that could preempt failure. With this foresight, maintenance can be scheduled at ideal times, parts ordered just-in-time, and disruption minimized—translating into cost savings and improved productivity.

The notion extends beyond manufacturing. In logistics, digital twins of delivery networks forecast optimal routes based on weather, traffic, and cargo conditions, resulting in fuel savings and timely deliveries. In the energy sector, the predictive prowess of digital twins refinements resource allocation on power grids, conserving energy and preventing costly outages.

Optimized Processes: The Symphony of Integration

Yet, the power of digital twins extends beyond mere prediction; it lies in the orchestration of optimized processes. By harmonizing workflows and synchronizing operations, digital twins transform the conventional into the optimized.

For instance, in production environments, digital twins offer clarity on process bottlenecks, suggesting reroutes of resources to where they are needed most, thereby eliminating inefficiencies. They also facilitate the simulation of process modifications, allowing operations to be fine-tuned before any changes are made to physical setups—ensuring disruption-free improvements.

Reacting dynamically to changes ensures that businesses not only maintain rhythm through strife, but dance seamlessly through fluctuations. An aerospace manufacturer might employ digital twins to redesign assembly workflows when a novel component is introduced, with simulations detailing the specific impacts on speed, quality, and cost—a far cry from traditional trial-and-error methodologies.

The Lean Enterprise: Cost Reduction Through Insight

Cost efficiency is the mantra of every enterprise, and digital twins make substantial contributions to this ever-pertinent goal.   By reducing waste, conserving resources, and streamlining operations, digital twins enable businesses to peel back layers of hidden costs that quietly erode profitability.

Achieving lean operations involves meticulous attention to resource use, and digital twins provide clarity to achieve such precision.   From evaluating energy consumption in complex HVAC systems to analyzing inventory redundancy in sprawling warehouses, digital twins identify squandered resources and suggest routes to efficiency. This not only slashes operational costs but aligns with broader sustainability goals—a synthesis of economics and ethics.

Additionally, in spaces like retail, digital twins can optimize supply chains, guiding strategic stock placements and minimizing costly overages and shortages, enhancing both efficiency and customer satisfaction.

Continuous Improvement: The Kaizen of the Digital Age

Akin to the Japanese philosophy of Kaizen, where incremental, continual improvement guides greatness, digital twins enable the modern enterprise to embrace an ethos of constant enhancement.

Through iterative analytics and feedback loops, digital

twins provide a testing ground for new ideas—be they process enhancements or product innovations—allowing refinement through digital trial before physical application. This approach not only improves current functions but facilitates innovation, ensuring that organizations are adaptable and future-ready.

For example, a telecommunications provider might use digital twins to virtually upgrade network protocols, stress-test bandwidth allocations, and introduce features without risking service interruptions—a testament to the power of proactive innovation.

Real-World Examples: Proving Ground and Paradigm Shift

In industries embracing digital twins, the results speak volumes. Rolls-Royce, known for its precision engineering, employs digital twins to revolutionize jet engine maintenance, transforming what was once time-consuming and costly into a streamlined process that predicts wear and guides servicing at minimal impact to flight schedules.

Similarly, Siemens has integrated digital twin solutions across its manufacturing facilities worldwide, resulting in significant reductions in waste and operational downtime. Through insights gained from virtual models that testify to real-world conditions, Siemens effects a level of process optimization that enhances output without increasing input—an industrial elixir of productivity.

Conclusion: A Vision of Optimized Potential

In the colorful mosaic of operational advancement, digital twins offer a potent brush: one where efficiency and insight merge, guiding businesses away from the morass of waste and toward the high plateau of refined achievement. Through digital twins, operational workflows are

101

not just managed but optimized, costs are not just reduced but eradicated, and potentials are not just reached
but exceeded.

As digital twins continue to expand their influence
across industries, their capability to clarify, inform,
and innovate will ensure that enterprises remain sharp,
efficient, and resilient in an ever-evolving landscape
of opportunity.   Digital twins thus act not merely as
tools but as partners in discovering paths to excellence,
illuminating the road to a future defined by perpetual
improvement and enduring success.

5.2   Improved Decision-Making

Consider the complexities of decision-making, the
intricate dance of uncertainty and intuition that has
challenged leaders, explorers, and strategists for
centuries. Every decision, however mundane, is fraught
with possibilities—a spectrum of outcomes woven with
threads of what if and what might be. As technology
surges forth with rapid strides, the digital twin emerges
as a beacon of clarity, charting a course through the fog
of indecision by providing a vista laden with insight
and foresight.

A Historical Dive into Decision-Making

Historically, decision-making rehearsed its nuanced
choreography with an orchestra of intuition, experience,
and available data.   From kings who dispatched
explorers with little more than maps marked by hearsay,
to industrialists who responded to market whims with
informed guesses, decisions have lingered somewhere
between art and science. But as the stakes heightened
with scales global and intricacies complex, a shift
began—a shift catalyzed by the power of data and the

dawn of simulation.

Enter digital twins, the modern-day digital oracles, whose origin story harks back to fundamental attempts at modeling and prediction in disciplines such as meteorology and operations research. Much like ancient seers who deciphered weather patterns etched in the stars, today's digital twins unravel data threads to forecast outcomes, paving the way for informed decision-making draped in precision.

The Twin Lens: Seeing Beyond the Surface

Central to the power of digital twins in decision-making is their ability to create virtual replicas of not just objects, but systems, processes, and environments—monitoring real-time data streams and synthesizing historical records to construct a fully interactive model.

Imagine urban planners visualizing traffic flow, infrastructure impacts, and environmental harmony through city-scale digital twins. These digital facsimiles simulate the effects of proposed road networks, transit systems, or residential expansions, allowing decision-makers to trial options, foresee consequences, and refine strategies without breaking ground.

Equipped with these insights, city planners transform conjectural proposals into actionable blueprints, ensuring that urban growth dovetails seamlessly with sustainability and livability goals—a far cry from the trial-and-error methods of yesteryears.

A New Dawn for Data-Driven Decisions

In the age of information, when data is veritably abundant, the greatest challenge lies in interpretation. Digital twins stand tall as analytical titans, employing machine-learning algorithms alongside simulations to traverse the data deluge, spotlight patterns, diagnose anomalies, and distill actionable intelligence.

Take the healthcare sector, where digital twins offer enlightened decision-making regarding patient treatment plans. Doctors can simulate myriad therapy scenarios through patient-specific digital twins— anticipating response variability, adverse reactions, and optimal dosages informed by past data and predictive models. These insights permit personalization and precision, enabling clinicians and patients to envision a clearer, more confident path to healing.

Industries such as manufacturing benefit equally as digital twins integrate with supply chains to forecast demand fluctuations, predict inventory needs, and align production schedules. The capability to visualize and maneuver around supply bottlenecks means businesses can adapt nimbly, optimizing output while minimizing risk—a testament to foresight redefined by digital acumen.

Enhanced Risk Management: Navigating the Unknown with Confidence

Decision-making thrives at the crossroads of possibility and risk, where every choice is imbued with potential opportunity and peril. Here, digital twins act as vigilant sentinels, simulating outcomes to gauge and even neutralize potential dangers.

Consider the safety protocols of the aviation industry, which rely on digital twins to simulate emergency scenarios. By assessing and validating varying responses— be they pilot actions, mechanical adjustments, or passenger behaviors—digital twins enhance preparedness and refine emergency procedures without the grim pull of a real-world crisis.

Similarly, financial institutions harness digital twins

to model market scenarios, evaluating investment strategies and risk exposures. By simulating recessions, booms, and economic conditions, these simulations empower financial strategists to make decisions that are judiciously hedged against uncertainty, ensuring stability amidst market turbulence.

Fostering Innovation: The Catalyst of Creativity

Beyond streamlining processes and minimizing risks, digital twins hold the enchanting promise of fostering innovation. Through immersive simulation environments, decision-makers have the latitude to experiment with unconventional ideas, evaluate their implications, and iterate towards breakthrough solutions.

In the automotive industry, for instance, digital twins enable engineers to test futuristic vehicle concepts without physical prototypes, exploring alternative energy sources, aerodynamic tweaks, and automated systems. This creative sandbox is where revolution meets realization—a proving ground for invention, illuminated by the clarity of digital insight.

Challenges and Considerations: A Balanced Perspective

Despite the illumination offered by digital twins, decision-makers must navigate challenges of dependency and data fidelity. As decisions increasingly lean on digital insights, the necessity of ensuring data accuracy and model integrity grows paramount, lest decisions wander astray on errant simulations.

Moreover, the nuanced balance between machine guidance and human intuition must be preserved. It is the unique human spark that questions, challenges, and sometimes defies conventional wisdom—qualities that meld with digital twins to cultivate synergistic decision-making that is as inspired as it is informed.

Real-World Triumphs: Harnessing the Power of Twins

Industries demonstrating the transformative power of digital twins abound.   In logistics, companies like DHL deploy digital twin models to optimize delivery networks, navigating complexities of supply chain disruptions through real-time data insights—an enactment of efficiency and timeliness.

Utilities, too, utilize digital twins to balance grid loads, predict energy demands, and seamlessly integrate renewable resources—preserving transparency in decision-making while advancing towards greener ambitions.

The Pathway Forward: Decisions Digitally Empowered

In a world where the complexity of decisions often mirrors labyrinthine paths, digital twins shine as digital cartographers, mapping routes ripe with potential—a compass guiding us toward strategic foresight rather than retrospective remedy.

The narrative of improved decision-making symphonizes seamlessly with the quest for understanding, as digital twins, shifting from promise to praxis, offer a palette from which clarity is drawn and complexities simplified.   They present a vista where evolution harmonizes with knowledge, driving societies toward socially attuned and economically conducive futures— the serene intersection of wisdom and whimsy.

Within this landscape of enlightened governance is where imagination collides with insight, where the domain of the hypothetical offers answers to the profound queries of modern development—reminding us that in the dance of decisions, digital twins stand not only as partners but as harbingers of an eloquent, empowered, and empathetic era.

5.3 Scalability and Flexibility

In the ever-shifting landscapes of technology and industry, scalability and flexibility emerge as pivotal cornerstones upon which the architecture of the digital age is built. In a world where change is the only constant, digital twins stand as paragons of adaptability, offering capabilities that transcend static models and rigid frameworks. They evolve in scope and function, reshaping themselves to meet the diverse demands and dynamics of a multifaceted global stage.

A Historical Prelude to Adaptability

The concept of scalability is not new; it is woven into the fabric of human evolution. From the ancient trade routes that expanded into the Silk Road, stretching across continents, to the Industrial Revolution's factories that transformed from humble workshops into sprawling behemoths of productivity, scalability has been a relentless quest: how to do more, reach further, and expand potential without losing integrity.

Similarly, flexibility has danced through history as the quiet muse of innovation. The capacity to pivot in response to unfolding unpredictabilities has been pivotal in survival, from nomadic tribes adapting to shifting ecosystems to industries adjusting to the technological tsunamis of the digital era.

In this rich tradition of adaptability, digital twins become both torchbearer and exemplar, empowering industries to scale effortlessly while maintaining an agile presence, pivoting along multiple axes as necessary.

107

The Elastic Nature of Digital Twins

At the heart of digital twins' scalability and flexibility is their digital quintessence: unlike physical systems chained by materials and geography, digital twins thrive in a boundless virtual realm. This elasticity—a freedom from physical limitations—allows digital twins to expand and adapt in lockstep with organizational needs, whether scaling up to encompass complex ecosystems or pivoting to address niche applications.

Imagine an automotive company utilizing digital twins for vehicle design, production, and testing. As market demands shift or new technologies emerge, the digital twin can effortlessly integrate additional data streams and simulations, testing new hypotheses or accommodating novel components with ease. The flexibility inherent in this approach ensures that the company remains at the cutting edge, always ready to respond to change with agility and confidence.

Beyond Initial Implementations: Expanding Horizons

Digital twins provide scalability that transcends individual objects to entire systems or enterprises. The energy sector exemplifies this capability, where digital twins monitor not only individual components like turbines or solar panels but scale to encompass entire grids. They predict energy loads, balance supply and demand, and integrate renewable resources across vast geographies, from bustling metropolitan hubs to remote rural locales.

In industries like healthcare, digital twins begin with patient-specific applications before scaling to broader healthcare systems. They model hospital operations, track resource allocation, and synchronize logistics across multiple sites, turning data into a powerful catalyst for improved patient outcomes and operational efficiency. This multiscale adaptability transforms organizational capabilities without imposing disruptive pressures on existing systems.

Flexibility: Navigating Emotional Intelligence in Technology

While scalability often speaks to size and capacity, flexibility connotes the ability to shift direction, accommodate new variables, and support nuanced interactions. In a rapidly evolving technological milieu, digital twins bring a dimension of digital emotional intelligence, adapting not just in physical or procedural terms but also in empathy-fueled understanding.

Consider the emergence of smart cities, where digital twins manage water distribution, waste management, and transportation networks. These digital ecosystems respond dynamically to citizen needs and environmental pressures, seamlessly adjusting services and infrastructure to reflect changing conditions or demographic trends.

By embracing a holistic understanding of the intricacies of urban life, digital twins help create responsive urban environments that prioritize quality of life. This flexibility redefines urban management from the unforeseeable burdens of growth to the anticipatory grace of seamless adaptation.

The Pioneering Role of Cloud Platforms

Underpinning the scalability and flexibility of digital twins are cloud platforms that provide the infrastructure necessary to store and process vast quantities of data from multiple sources. Cloud computing eliminates the need for traditional constraints, offering virtually infinite resources to scale and adapt functionalities on demand.

109

Retail giants like Amazon harness cloud-supported digital twins to fine-tune supply chain dynamics, anticipate consumer preferences, and optimize logistics operations. This infrastructure allows them to modulate operations with seasons, cycles, or trends, delighting customers and achieving operational fluidity irrespective of external circumstances.

Inspiration from Biology: Learning from Nature's Models

The potential of digital twins mirrors nature's models of scalability and flexibility—the way organisms grow and adapt to environments through evolution or the way ecosystems self-regulate in response to external changes. Biological networks offer insightful parallels, inspiring the design and function of digital twins.

Consider the analogy of a tree, scaling effortlessly upward and outward while flexing in response to gusts of wind or seasonal forces. Digital twins, in turn, embody a similar duality: poised for growth yet grounded in resilience, always capable of reacting to present conditions while preparing for future possibilities.

Maximizing Potential: Real-World Applications and Benefits

Leveraging scalability and flexibility transforms industries, offering tangible benefits such as enhanced efficiency, optimal resource utilization, and rapid innovation. Retail, transportation, manufacturing, and healthcare sectors derive significant value in scaling operations to accommodate market shifts, fostering agility to seize emerging opportunities, and weaving flexibility into employee practices and cultures.

Airline industries, for example, employ digital twins to track fleet performance while simulating future flight paths, accommodating variable conditions such as weather, fuel costs, or passenger fluctuations. This strategic modulation maximizes profitability while preserving reliability and safety standards.

Furthermore, the adaptability cultivated by digital twins transforms supply chains into living networks, where logistics evolve organically based on real-time information, regulatory shifts, or consumer behavior insights. This poise in adaptability creates superior customer experiences and operational resilience in an interconnected world.

Challenges and Future Directions: Pathway to Expansive Possibilities

Despite their promise, deploying digital twins requires navigating pitfalls such as data silos, security vulnerabilities, or interoperability concerns. A collaborative approach, engaging stakeholders across industries and disciplines, cultivates environments where digital twins can flourish without compromise.

Future directions will likely focus on enhancing predictive analytics, exploring inter-twin synergies, and advancing artificial intelligence integration, propelling digital twins into the forefront of technological innovation, from cradle to scalability and flexibility unimagined.

Within the synergy of scalability and flexibility lies the potential to reimagine what industries can achieve. Digital twins transform the static limits of today into the adaptive frontiers of tomorrow, empowering organizations to engage with transformative opportunities.

As these digital companions blaze pathways into the future, they emphasize that the journey of resilience and dynamism isn't solely technological—it's a dialogue between imagination, creativity, and insight. Industries that embrace digital twins herald change with joy, crafting landscapes of unparalleled productivity and progress through initiatives that stand agile and expansive.

In the echoes of their adaptability lies a vision of enduring synergy—scalability's reach united with flexibility's response—ushering a quintessence of purpose and technologic possibility, readied not just to meet today's challenges but to flourish within tomorrow's promise.

5.4   Technical and Infrastructure Challenges

As the digital age continues to unfold, digital twins stand at the cutting edge of technological advancement, promising a future of interconnected systems and seamless integration.   Yet, beneath the sheen of progress lies a tapestry of challenges—technical and infrastructural hurdles that must be adeptly navigated to truly harness the transformative potential of digital twins. This exploration will delve into these challenges, revealing the labyrinth of complexities that accompany the adoption and implementation of this pioneering technology.

A Forerunner's Challenge: The Path to Integration

Historically, technological revolutions have been accompanied by growing pains.   From the telegraph wire tangles of the 19th century to the early internet's slow dial-up connections, each leap forward has been marked by its own set of trials.   Digital twins are no different.   One of the most formidable challenges they face is integration—the art of unifying disparate systems into a cohesive whole.

In many enterprises, systems have evolved over decades, creating a patchwork of legacy technologies and proprietary solutions. Integrating digital twins requires untangling these webs, ensuring seamless communication across platforms that were never designed to converse. This challenge extends beyond coding compatibility to encompass cultural and procedural changes within organizations, often steered by technological inertia.

Take the manufacturing sector, for example. Factories equipped with dated machinery may struggle to integrate sensors and deploy real-time data analytics necessary for digital twin operations. This task demands not only technological upgrades but also meticulous strategy, aligning new capabilities with existing workflows—a delicate dance of evolution and tradition.

Data Integration and Interoperability: The Double-Edged Sword

Data—the lifeblood of digital twins—poses its own set of integration challenges. While data offers opportunities for insight and optimization, the sheer volume and variety of data generated complicates seamless integration. Ensuring data quality, consistency, and availability across systems strains current computational frameworks, requiring robust infrastructures capable of managing the flow and storage efficiently.

Interoperability is another crucial factor, defined by the ability of systems to exchange and process data across diverse platforms and formats. Across industries, interoperability issues arise when digital twins attempt to unify data from siloed environments—each with its own schema, protocols, and operating procedures.

Consider smart cities, where urban planners face the task of integrating data from transport, utilities, healthcare, and public safety systems. Each domain speaks its own digital dialect, necessitating sophisticated middleware solutions and standards to ensure fluid data interchange and actionable intelligence. Progress hinges on collaboration among vendors and stakeholders to agree upon open standards, fostering an ecosystem where digital twins can thrive without bottlenecks.

Infrastructure: Building the Digital Foundations

The implementation of digital twins requires a robust underlying infrastructure—akin to constructing a skyscraper that rests on a solid foundation. Without it, even the most sophisticated digital twin is destined to falter. This foundational complexity is multi-dimensional, encompassing computational power, data storage capabilities, and network bandwidth.

High-performance computing solutions are essential to process the vast datasets that digital twins analyze in real-time. This dependency reinforces the need for investments in cutting-edge servers, GPUs, and cloud-based platforms. Likewise, scalable cloud storage ensures data permanence and accessibility, supporting the continuous flow of real-time updates and historical analytics.

Bandwidth limitations pose another infrastructural challenge, especially in contexts where vast quantities of data must traverse global networks. Real-time applications are particularly reliant on low-latency connections, necessitating efficient network architectures that balance speed, reliability, and security.

In the automotive industry, as connected vehicles gather and transmit data to their digital twins, comprehensive 5G infrastructure emerges as a vital enabler, reducing latency and amplifying the capacity to handle complex simulation and analytic tasks—shaping the contours of future mobility solutions.

114

Security and Privacy: Guardians of the Digital Realm

Amid the technological intricacies of digital twins, safeguarding security and privacy becomes paramount. As these digital replicas continuously exchange sensitive data, establishing robust cyber defenses ensures that vulnerabilities are minimized, and malicious threats are repelled.

This challenge is magnified when considering sectors such as healthcare, where patient data forms the nucleus of digital twin operations. Ensuring data privacy involves implementing end-to-end encryption, secure authentication paths, and compliance with evolving regulatory landscapes such as the GDPR or HIPAA.

Secured data access controls, rigorous auditing mechanisms, and penetration testing are critical components of a proactive security strategy, fostering an environment of trust and reliability for all stakeholders engaged with digital twin systems.

Overcoming Skill Gaps: Equipping the Workforce

As industries wade deeper into the waters of digital twin technology, the need for a skilled workforce capable of adeptly implementing and managing these solutions becomes evident. Bridging this skill gap is an intrinsic challenge, requiring investment in education and training to equip employees with necessary expertise.

Engaging with educational institutions, rolling out upskilling initiatives, and fostering a culture of continuous learning are strategies employed by organizations preparing their workforce for the digital era. Moreover, fostering interdisciplinary collaboration aids in melding traditional industry knowledge with digital prowess—ensuring that digital twins are effectively utilized and their capabilities fully realized.

Commitment to Challenges: A Blueprint for Progress

Navigating technical and infrastructural challenges is not a solitary journey; it requires collaboration, commitment, and an innovative mindset. Key industry figures and technology providers must work in tandem, developing solutions that pave the way for seamless digital twin integrations.

Examples of such collaboration include cross-industry consortiums focused on developing interoperability standards and cooperative initiatives with state and local governments to modernize infrastructure. These partnerships herald the formation of robust frameworks, reducing complexity and fostering an ethos of collective progress.

The Bright Frontier: Embracing Opportunity

While the challenges of implementing digital twins are significant, they are not insurmountable. Ably addressed, these obstacles transform into opportunities, enabling industries to unlock new dimensions of efficiency, insight, and innovation.

In addressing these challenges with strategic foresight, businesses not only overcome the technical and infrastructure hurdles but are rewarded with the capacity to innovate and succeed within an ever-evolving technological landscape—turning promise into practice and innovating for tomorrow, today. As digital twins continue to weave their way into the very fabric of industry, they offer us a future not just imagined, but achievable—one in which technology empowers by streamlining complexities and catalyzing progress across every field it touches.

5.5 Investment and Skill Barriers

As the promise of digital twins pivots from ethereal allure into concrete value, it stands at the cusp of mainstream adoption by industries worldwide. However, not every organization is ensconced in this promise. The realization of digital twin technology requires both financial investment and human resource development. In navigating these investment and skill barriers, businesses stand to unlock a reservoir of potential or risk relegating themselves to the sidelines of innovation.

Historical Perspectives: Investing in Change

The dance between innovation and investment is as old as industry itself. From the mechanization of textile looms during the Industrial Revolution to the capital-intensive rise of Silicon Valley, each leap forward has demanded a formidable outlay of resources—both fiscal and intellectual.

Historically, these investments have not been devoid of risk. Innovators from James Watt to Thomas Edison juggled financial constraints with the imperative to push the boundaries of what was possible. Their ventures often teetered on the precipice of success and insolvency, ultimately choosing to stake resources on the promise of future returns—a narrative that echoingly parallels today's pursuit of digital twin implementation.

Financial Investment: The Cost of Opportunity

To capitalize on the transformative power of digital twins, organizations must navigate the financial landscape. Implementing this technology is not just about acquiring new software; it is about embedding a comprehensive solution that redefines operations. Such initiatives require an upfront investment in technology infrastructure, data management systems, and integration protocols.

The total cost of ownership can be considerable. From procuring state-of-the-art sensors for data collection to investing in cloud platforms that provide computational muscle, the financial implications are multifaceted. For small to medium enterprises, the barrier of entry may seem steep, potentially overshadowing the perceived benefits.

For instance, a mid-sized manufacturing firm contemplating digital twin adoption might weigh the outlay for upgrading machinery with embedded IoT devices against the anticipated gains in efficiency and reduced downtime. While budget constraints could curb enthusiasm, a strategic investment view—illustrating long-term cost savings, optimized resource use, and competitive advantage—can be compelling, prompting companies to cross the chasm from reluctance to embrace.

Skill Gaps: Building the Workforce of Tomorrow

Parallel to financial considerations is the challenge of skill deficits. Digital twins are sophisticated, multifaceted, and interconnected tools requiring specialized expertise not just to build but also to leverage fully. The burgeoning demand for a digitally literate workforce capable of integrating data analytics, system modeling, and IoT technologies with industry-specific knowledge is acute.

This calls for a paradigm shift in workforce development, where education and skills training are prioritized to align with evolving technological landscapes. Organizations must engage in structured training programs to upskill their existing workforce and attract fresh talent adept in data science, AI, simulation, and related technologies.

Consider health systems adopting digital twins, where clinical staff must now collaborate with data scientists to model and interpret patient-specific simulations. Developing these interdisciplinary competencies involves partnerships with educational institutions, professional development opportunities, and a commitment to continuous learning.

Navigating the Investment Conundrum

Organizations grappling with investment challenges must weigh immediate costs against long-term organizational transformation. This calculus requires adeptness beyond balance sheets, factoring qualitative improvements such as enhanced decision-making, agility, and resilience.

A phased implementation strategy can mitigate financial burdens—beginning with pilot projects or targeted investment in high-impact areas can yield early wins and quantify benefits, which in turn fosters confidence for wider adoption. Collaborative initiatives, where costs and risks are shared with partners or stakeholders, are emerging as viable models to encourage strategic adoption without shouldering the financial weight alone.

For example, automotive giants may pilot digital twins in specific R&D areas, iterating successes across broader departments once value is demonstrated. This modular approach allows refinements to implementation strategies, ensuring that the full spectrum of benefits is gradually but effectively realized.

Bridging Skill Barriers: A Collaborative Effort

Addressing the skill barriers requires a coordinated effort, interweaving academia, industry, and government collaborations. Educational programs must expand beyond traditional curricula, integrating digital literacy, computational thinking, and domain-specific applications into core offerings.

Collaborative training efforts, such as apprenticeships, on-the-job training, and cross-disciplinary workshops, enhance practical skills and ensure industry-ready graduates. Moreover, fostering a culture of knowledge exchange within organizations, where experienced professionals mentor emerging talent, facilitates organic growth and propagation of expertise.

In the energy sector, for instance, utilities might partner with academic institutions to develop coursework specific to digital twin technologies, encompassing everything from grid management to cyber-physical systems—a preemptive stance to ensure the workforce is not just functional but leading-edge.

Overcoming Resistance: The Human Element

While investment and skill gaps pose tangible barriers, the human element also plays a critical role in the adoption journey. Resistance to change, rooted in fear of the unknown or the perceived complexity of new technologies, can stagnate progress. Addressing this requires visionary leadership—capable of articulately communicating the strategic value of digital twins and fostering an environment of trust and acceptance.

Empowering employees by including them in the adoption process—from evaluation to implementation—reinforces commitment and aligns aspirations. Success stories, anecdotal evidence, or case studies illustrating tangible benefits can be rallying cries that unite organizations toward a shared transformational agenda.

Looking to the Horizon: The Promise of Progress

Despite the barriers of investment and skill, the horizon offers hope, illustrated by successful implementations where digital twins catalyze transformative outcomes. Companies that invest strategically and cultivate skills dynamically are poised to capture the immense potential inherent in digital twin technologies.

Indeed, digital twins promise to transcend their initial capital and intellectual costs by unlocking efficiencies, innovations, and competitive advantages that ripple across industry sectors. From optimized operations to enhanced customer experiences, the tangible and intangible returns extend far beyond initial expenditures—a testament to the foresighted brilliance of investment made wisely.

It is in the symphony of industrial evolution, where investment and skill barriers are not merely hurdles to overcome; they are clarion calls urging organizations to evolve with purpose, courage, and clarity. The path to digital twin adoption requires commitment to vision and action—encompassed in a philosophy where tomorrow's opportunities are crafted today through thoughtful investment and meticulous skill development.

As industries journey forth into this promising frontier, they underscore an enduring legacy: where innovation thrives, investment is justified, and skills empower the future—a future where digital twins become not only technological marvels but harmonious participants in the concert of progress.

Chapter 6

The Role of Data and Analytics in Digital Twins

Data and analytics are the cornerstone of digital twin functionality, enabling accurate replication and real-time analysis of physical systems. Effective data acquisition, management, and storage systems support the seamless operation of digital twins. Advanced analytical tools, including machine learning and AI, transform raw data into actionable insights, facilitating predictive modeling and optimization. Ensuring data quality and security is critical to maintaining reliability and performance. This chapter explores how data and analytics drive the capabilities of digital twins, highlighting their role in enhancing understanding and operational outcomes.

6.1   Data Acquisition Techniques

In the age of digital ubiquity, data is often heralded as the "new oil," a valuable resource driving the engine of contemporary technological marvels. Yet unlike oil, data's value isn't bound to its scarcity but to its ability to reveal insights—an accomplishment reliant on sophisticated data acquisition techniques. For digital twins, these techniques serve as the backbone, facilitating the creation of accurate, real-time replicas of physical systems. By capturing the essence of the tangible world through streams of data, digital twins offer a portal into enhanced understanding and predictive analytics.

Tracing the Roots: A Historical Perspective on Data Acquisition

The journey of data acquisition dates back to antiquity, where early civilizations collected basic environmental and astronomical data to understand seasons or forecast eclipses—an endeavor vesting humans with a semblance of control over an unpredictable world. Fast-forward to the 20th century, and we witness the evolution of instrumentation, wherein sensors plant their roots in scientific discovery and industrial monitoring.

From the heart of Apollo missions, where sensors captured spacecraft telemetry, to the proliferation of automated control systems in manufacturing, data acquisition matured into a cornerstone of modern innovation. Today, it reaches its zenith through the seamless integration of sensors, IoT, and advanced networking—melding the physical and digital into an operatic duet.

Sensor Networks: The Sensory Sentinels

Central to data acquisition for digital twins are sensor networks, often described as the sensory organs that translate real-world phenomena into digital data. These sensory sentinels are as diverse as the applications they facilitate—from temperature probes monitoring delicate environments to accelerometers gauging the motion of vehicles.

Consider a smart building networked with temperature, humidity, and occupancy sensors. This interconnected system provides granular data, painting a comprehensive picture of environmental conditions within the building. This precision enables building managers to optimize energy consumption and enhance occupant comfort, illustrating how sensor networks are more than passive observers—they are active contributors to systems optimization.

IoT Integration: Bridging the Physical and Digital

With its potential for ubiquitous connectivity, the Internet of Things (IoT) stands as a transformative pillar of contemporary data acquisition, bridging the physical and digital with flair. IoT devices, ingrained with sensors and connectivity, accumulate vast datasets that feed digital twins' hunger for real-time information.

Illustrating this is the realm of agriculture, where IoT-integrated sensors monitor soil health, moisture levels, and weather conditions. These data streams converge within digital twins—virtual farmlands dotted with real-time metrics—enabling farmers to make informed decisions about irrigation, fertilization, and crop selection. By leveraging IoT, agriculture transcends tradition, embracing precision as a virtuous endeavor.

Industrial Applications: The Pulse of Production

In the industrial arena, data acquisition techniques find profound application, offering pathways to efficiency and foresight beyond the reach of traditional methodologies. Advanced sensor technologies monitor vibrations in machinery, providing not just snapshots of operation but holistic narratives of performance trajectories.

Manufacturers like General Electric embed sensors within jet engines, creating digital twins that mirror an engine's every heartbeat. These sensors detect minuscule anomalies—variations in temperature or pressure—that might precede maintenance needs. This vigilance transforms maintenance from reactive to predictive, reducing downtime and preserving operational integrity.

Overcoming Challenges: Data Quality and Calibration

While the orchestra of sensor networks and IoT plays harmoniously, challenges persist in ensuring data quality—a necessity for deriving actionable insights. Calibration of sensors, for instance, is paramount to remove discrepancies and inconsistencies that might skew results—a task that amalgamates art and science in perfect measure.

Furthermore, as data flows from myriad sources, validating its accuracy and contextualizing it within its environment becomes imperative. Addressing data integrity involves deploying advanced algorithms for filtering noise, detecting outliers, and reconstructing high-fidelity datasets fit for simulation and analysis.

Stakeholders and Collaborations: The Collaborative Canvas

Data acquisition techniques for digital twins are no longer confined within siloed entities. Diverse stakeholders—from technology vendors to service providers—engage collaboratively to enhance the value propositions of sensor networks and IoT systems. Cross-industry initiatives work to standardize data protocols and frameworks, promoting interoperability and easing data integration.

While the automotive industry, for instance, benefits from sensor manufacturers' advancements, it reciprocally pushes for enhanced connectivity solutions and telematics standards. This symbiotic relationship encourages a fertile ground where innovation flourishes, riding on the coattails of collaborative ingenuity.

Evolving Technologies: The Future of Data Acquisition

As the horizon of data acquisition stretches into the future, emerging technologies offer a lens into possibilities yet unimagined. Quantum sensors—a frontier of sensitivity—promise unparalleled detection capabilities, enriching digital twins with data streams of unprecedented granularity.

Additionally, edge computing enables decentralized data processing—ushering in real-time analytics at the source of data generation, curtailing latency concerns and enhancing responsiveness. These advancements signal a world where digital twins are empowered to evolve in tandem with their environments, maintaining fidelity through dynamic recalibration.

Applications Beyond Industry: The Human Spectrum

Data acquisition techniques not only empower industries but extend into personal realms, enhancing lives through health monitoring and environmental awareness. Smart wearables use sensors to acquire health metrics, constructing digital twins of individuals that offer healthcare professionals a comprehensive view of well-being.

These digital representations facilitate proactive health interventions, exemplifying how data acquisition extends beyond technical marvels into the heart of human experience, promoting wellness through insightful analytics.

Conclusion: Encompassing Complexity and Insight

The sophisticated tapestry of data acquisition techniques supporting digital twins heralds an era where complexity embraces clarity, fostering systems deeply attuned to their environments and stakeholders. By leveraging sensor networks, IoT integration, and collaborative frameworks, digital twins reveal informed vistas that guide industries, improve lives, and safeguard environments.

As these techniques continue to mature, the lessons of historical evolutions urge us to creatively leverage technology, ensuring that data acquisition serves not just as a facilitator of digital twins but as an enabler of informed and inspired futures—a future where our digital reality refines the intricate symphony of human aspiration and technological progress.

6.2   Data Management and Storage

In the grand hallways of the digital age, data serves as both the weary traveler and the voyager's most treasured map—leading us to insights untold and guiding us through complexities unseen. As such, in the realm of digital twins, data management and storage stand paramount, orchestrating a delicate balance between keeping information secure and making it accessible, reliable, and ready for interpretation. At its core, this is a tale of conservation and curation.

From Scrolls to Servers: The Evolution of Data Custody

Our quest to store and manage information is deeply etched into the annals of history. Ancient scribes inscribed clay tablets, while medieval monks painstakingly copied manuscripts—each generation inventing storied sanctuaries for their wisdom. The narrative reshaped itself with Gutenberg's press, the filing systems of the Victorian era, and eventually, the digital archives that characterize our modern world.

As the digital universe exploded, so too did the data we generated—pixels and pulses descending as showers of information on industries unprepared for such wealth. What followed was an arms race of technology, as businesses sought to keep apace with burgeoning storage demands—a battle for bytes no longer waged in filing cabinets, but on servers and in the cloud.

The Pillars of Data Management

Effective data management for digital twins encompasses several key facets. At its essence, data management ensures that the cascades of information feeding digital twins transform from chaotic torrents into organized tributaries that can be readily monitored, updated, and queried.

- **Data Structuring and Organization**

  Like a library without catalogues, unstructured data is formidable in its unwieldiness. Thus, the first step in data management is structuring it—ordering it as a librarian would shelves filled with diverse tomes. Here, database tools and data architectures are called upon to ensure data is formatted not just for storage but for retrieval, whether housed in on-premises servers or breezing through cloud-computing constructs.

- **Data Integration**

  In a world where data flows freely between multiple channels, integration ensures seamless interaction among sources, systems, and platforms. This orchestration ensures digital twins receive the comprehensive, real-time

129

information necessary to model and simulate accurately. Through data integration tools and middleware, businesses align disparate data streams to create holistic portrayals of complex realities.

- **Data Governance**

  Data democracy brings with it the challenge of governance—the stewardship of data policies, standards, and roles that guarantee data integrity throughout its lifecycle. Ensuring protocols are adhered to is crucial as decisions rely on the data being genuine and trustworthy, and herein resides the not-so-quiet guardian role played by governance frameworks.

Storied Storage Solutions: A Tech-Ballet

Data storage has evolved into a multifaceted discipline geared towards ensuring accessibility without sacrificing security—a tech-ballet danced across multi-layered servers.

- **On-premises vs. Cloud Storage**

  While traditional on-premises servers remain viable, the flexibility of cloud storage is undeniable—a siren song promising elasticity, scalability, and availability on demand. Cloud technologies enable the storage of vast data volumes, allowing organizations to seamlessly scale storage capacities in response to fluctuating requirements.

  Consider retail giants who deploy hybrid storage solutions to manage customer and sales data, processing it on-premises yet distributing it through cloud networks to support global operations. The fusion of technologies ensures that data is both centralized for control and distributed for operational fluidity.

- **Data Warehouses and Data Lakes**

  Specialized storage solutions, such as data warehouses and data lakes, play distinct yet complementary roles. Data warehouses are structured environments prioritizing speed and efficiency—suited for processed data used in business analytics. Conversely, data lakes serve as expansive reservoirs for raw, unprocessed data ripe for diving into exploratory analysis and future innovation.

- **Data Archiving**

  Like preserving rare manuscripts, data archiving ensures that data retains its value long after its initial use. By cataloging historical data, organizations treasure foundational information, enabling retrospection and long-term analysis. The cloud adds a unique facet—offering cost-effective long-term storage solutions without traditional spatial constraints.

Enhancing Data Accessibility and Reliability

To unlock the potential of data, accessibility is crucial, and reliability must be assured. Efficient data management ensures that needed data is only a click away, enabling digital twins to synthesize simulations and scenarios without interruptions.

To bolster reliability, redundancy measures, such as data mirroring, replication, and backup systems, become essential. Data redundancy means that if one server or data center fails, another can seamlessly take its place, ensuring digital twins keep functioning uninterrupted.

In finance, banking institutions leverage sophisticated redundancies to maintain unbroken access to transactional data—from branch records to real-time trading logs—ensuring digital twins continuously assess risk and liquidity in volatile ecosystems.

Data Security: The Watchful Custodian

In managing data's prolific flow, security emerges as both a shield and a sanctum. The emergence of digital twins, which rely on sensitive and mission-critical data, heightens the need for vigilant security measures throughout data processing and storage lifecycles.

Encryption protocols, access controls, and hyper-vigilant intrusion detection contribute to a well-defended data castle, eliminating vulnerabilities that cyber threats may exploit. Robust security not only preserves data confidentiality but also safeguards digital twins' operability—thus maintaining stakeholder trust and operational veracity.

Navigating Challenges: Sifting the Technical Frontier

Navigating the multifaceted challenges of data management and storage is formidable yet rewarding. Businesses must continuously adapt to evolving technologies and best practices, ensuring they remain nimble in a digital landscape entwined with perennial progress.

- **Scalability**

    As data volumes surge, scalability remains paramount. Solutions like cloud elasticity provide scalable infrastructure adaptable to the growing demands without infrastructure overhauls, ensuring data platforms grow in tandem with organizational needs.

- **Compliance**

  Adherence to regulatory compliance shapes data management strategies—dictating how data is collected, stored, and used. Industries from healthcare to finance align systems with regulations like GDPR and HIPAA, often adopting advanced auditing mechanisms to maintain compliance in data-intense environments.

Data management and storage find themselves in the eye of a digital storm—a crescendo of opportunity energized by insights yet to be gleaned. As organizations refine their data management strategies and storage architectures, the path ahead is one of continuous innovation.

In this ever-evolving panoply of digital possibility, the stewardship of data transcends historical custodianship, spurring forth a reality where digital twins become artifacts of understanding and exploration. This journey guides us toward new frontiers and broader horizons, where the power of data, deftly managed and wisely stored, illuminates the orchestration of innovation with radiant possibility—a possibility bounded only by the imagination and ambition of those daring enough to dream.

6.3 Analytical Tools and Technologies

Imagine having a crystal ball that can peer into the very essence of operations, predict complications before they materialize, and suggest pathways to optimal outcomes. In the world of digital twins, this crystal ball takes the form of analytical tools and technologies—sophisticated instruments that dissect the data deluge into manageable insights and actionable strategies. As digital twins

weave their tale across industries, these tools transform
invisible possibilities into tangible realities.

From Observation to Insight: A Historical Perspective

The quest for analytics is as ancient as humanity's desire
to make sense of the stars. Early sages and philosophers,
from Ptolemy to Da Vinci, sought patterns in the heavens
and art—attempts to predict the tides of fate and fortune.
In modern times, analytics evolved into systematic exploration with the advent of statistical models and computing capabilities.

The power of analytics experienced a resurgence in the
late 20th century, characterized by data mining and business intelligence that buoyed enterprises on the spring-
board of information technology. Today, as we voyage
into the era of digital domination, analytical tools stand
as sentinels of insight, guarding the interface between
data and decision-making, shaped by advancements in
artificial intelligence and machine learning.

Machine Learning and Artificial Intelligence: The Brain Behind the Twin

At the center of cutting-edge analytical tools are
machine learning (ML) and artificial intelligence
(AI)—technologies that propel digital twins into
the realm of cognitive ability.   Unlike traditional
programming, where rules are explicitly defined,
machine learning enables systems to discern patterns
and adapt autonomously through exposure to new
data.

Consider the automotive industry, where ML
algorithms within digital twins furnish real-time
diagnostics and predictive maintenance schedules.
These algorithms continuously analyze streams of
data from vehicle sensors, identifying anomalies or

performance deviations that might herald mechanical issues. Beyond reactive measures, AI-driven twins forecast future maintenance needs, optimizing service intervals and ensuring safety.

AI amplifies the capability of digital twins beyond simple replications, converting data into foresight-powered simulators capable of learning and refining operations based on historical and real-time inputs.

Natural Language Processing: Communicating with Clarity

Another technological spearhead is Natural Language Processing (NLP)—an AI branch that empowers computers to understand and interpret human language. Within the digital twin ecosystem, NLP facilitates intuitive interfaces, allowing users to converse with data analytics tools in everyday language without navigating complex coding landscapes.

In healthcare, NLP-equipped digital twins support clinicians by synthesizing disparate patient narratives, diagnostics, and treatment histories. Doctors ask questions in natural language, receiving insights drawn from extensive medical databases—ushering in an era of personalized patient care that speaks in humanistic terms.

Predictive and Prescriptive Analytics: Knowing and Acting

The genius of analytical tools lies in their progression from predictive to prescriptive analytics, advancing our ability to forecast outcomes and propose actions. Predictive analytics leverages historical data to build models that anticipate future events and trends, while prescriptive analytics integrates these forecasts to determine optimal responses.

In supply chain management, digital twins armed with

these analytics monitor production flows, inventory levels, and transportation routes to identify bottlenecks or potential disruptions. They simulate various scenarios, providing decision-makers with recommended actions that minimize risk while maximizing efficiency—a balanced dance of anticipation and action.

Static vs. Dynamic Models: Choosing the Right Lens

Analytics within digital twins operate through either static or dynamic models, each offering unique lenses into systems.

Static models represent a snapshot in time, ideal for evaluating structured systems or long-term trends where conditions remain relatively constant. Conversely, dynamic models are akin to an unfolding movie—capturing fluctuations, feedback, and evolution in real-time.

Manufacturing industries employ dynamic models to oversee assembly lines, adapting to real-time data inputs and adjusting processes on the fly—this ensures optimized throughput and seamless coordination even amidst unforeseen variability.

Visualization Tools: Painting Pictures with Data

The beauty of analytical insights is often best appreciated through visualization tools, translating abstract data patterns into tangible graphics, charts, and simulations. These tools ingeniously distill complexity into intuitive representations, supporting strategic interpretations and fostering collaboration across teams.

Digital twins in urban planning illustrate this vividly, where citywide data is mapped in 3D environments. Planners visualize traffic patterns, environmental impacts, and land use dynamics, exploring myriad development scenarios with visual clarity, ultimately crafting solutions that address community needs and enhance urban livability.

Edge Computing: Proximity with Precision

Edge computing represents an evolved domain in analytics by processing data closer to the source rather than relying on centralized data centers. This proximity empowers digital twins with speedier analytics and responses, particularly in scenarios requiring instantaneous decision-making.

Consider autonomous vehicles transmitting data to digital twin models for navigation and safety adjustments, all processed on-board through edge computing. This setup avoids latency and ensures real-time analytics—an automatic system that recalibrates based on proximity-processed insights.

Collaborative Platforms and Open Source Analytics

As the digital ecosystem burgeons, collaboration and open-source analytics become pivotal in democratizing access to analytical technologies. Shared platforms and open-source repositories catalyze innovation by allowing cross-industry collaboration and refinement without exorbitant costs.

Companies like Cloudera and Apache Spark engage communities with open-source data analytics frameworks, ensuring that organizations can leverage cutting-edge tools while contributing to a culture of shared advancement—a harmonious exchange of ideas that cultivates adaptive solutions.

The Ethical Landscape: Responsibility in Analytics

With great analytical power comes equally great responsibility. Ethical considerations touch every facet of data analytics, particularly as digital twins influence critical decisions impacting health, safety, and privacy.

Ensuring ethical standards in algorithm development, data interpretation, and insight application demands vigilance. Establishing transparent practices and clear accountability frameworks remains vital to sustaining trust and integrity in the intelligence derived from digital twins.

The Path Forward: Insights as Catalysts

In the tapestry of digital twin functionality, analytical tools and technologies illuminate pathways of possibility, transforming raw data into actionable intelligence— insights that empower industries, individuals, and societies to align aspirations with achievable realities.

The narrative of these analytical marvels is one of collaboration, reflection, and progress: a constellation of enlightened techniques and tools enhancing our perceptive potential. As they continue to evolve, these technologies will refine the contours of innovation, embellishing the story of digital twins with an elegance defined by curiosity, capability, and a ceaseless pursuit of understanding—a timeless and inevitable need that constantly beckons us forward.

6.4   Real-Time Analytics and Predictive Modeling

Picture, if you will, the seamless flow of data, cascading in torrents through digital channels, scrutinized not by human eye alone, but by automated allies capable of parsing every droplet in real-time. This is the realm of real-time analytics and predictive modeling—a domain where data is not a static artifact of the past, but a dynamic canvas revealing the emergent patterns of the present and the faint outlines of the future. In the age of digital twins, these capabilities achieve an apex of relevance, transforming raw information into coherent strategies and informed foresight.

A Historical Prelude: The Long View of Prediction

Predictions have continuously fascinated humankind, from ancient readings of celestial bodies to the almanacs forecasting climates for sowing crops. The historical journey of prediction unveils a symphony of intuition and emerging science, culminating in the analytical rigor of today's computational capabilities.

The Industrial Revolution marked the early stages of predictive analytics, using rudimentary statistical methods to foresee product demands and labor needs. This evolution was further invigorated by 20th-century computational advancements, transforming prediction from a speculative art into a strategic science—an ascension well illustrated by military logistics and economic forecasting tactics.

As we entered the digital era, real-time analytics crystallized into a hallmark of technological acumen—a divergence from past static sets towards an immediate, reactive mode of data interpretation. In this context, real-time analytics melds seamlessly with predictive modeling, offering not just an understanding of the immediate terrain but strategic navigation toward future horizons.

Real-Time Analytics: Sensing the Current

In the world of digital twins, real-time analytics is akin to the nervous system of a living organism, constantly evaluating and responding to environmental stimuli. By capturing data instantaneously, it provides an up-to-the-minute portrait of system performance and operational integrity.

Consider the bustling field of finance, where digital twins sweep through market data at lightning speed, identifying anomalies, trends, and opportunities. Real-time analytics allows traders to execute decisions with precision, timing trades to capitalize on fleeting market conditions, mitigating risks, and maximizing returns—a process that transcends human capability alone.

A compelling application lies within the manufacturing sector, where digital twins monitor factory floors, keenly sensing deviations from production norms. By identifying potential bottlenecks or equipment wear when they arise—rather than after—they facilitate immediate interventions, preserving machine health and ensuring operational consistency. It's akin to having a real-time pulse monitor that acts to rectify an erratic heartbeat before it escalates into a crisis.

Predictive Modeling: Strategizing Ahead

While real-time analytics highlights the present, predictive modeling peers into the veils of destiny, aligning data with statistical algorithms to forecast future scenarios. This capacity empowers stakeholders to anticipate trends, optimize resources, and ultimately navigate uncertainties with confidence.

Take energy management, where the confluence of digital twins and predictive models harmonizes energy consumption with utility provision. By forecasting energy loads, operators can strategically allocate resources, balancing supply and demand even as constraints shift. Moreover, predictive models enable wind farms to integrate meteorological forecasts, maximizing renewable energy potential while savvily addressing grid fluctuations.

Transportation systems, too, benefit from predictive foresight. In urban contexts, digital twins monitor real-time traffic patterns and simulate the impact of various infrastructural changes or policy interventions, guiding planners toward strategies that alleviate congestion and reduce environmental impacts.

Intertwined Futures: Real-Time Meets Predictive

Real-time analytics and predictive modeling operate not in isolation but in concert, a symbiotic dance where immediate insights craft prognostications and forecasts reclaim relevance through current data streams. Within digital twins, this partnership provides agile intelligence, transforming isolated data points into intricate webs of understanding.

A retail chain, for instance, utilizes digital twins to seamlessly coordinate inventory decisions based on current sales dynamics and anticipated consumer trends. Real-time analytics discern fluctuating purchase behaviors, while predictive models forecast seasonal demands—ensuring stores stock precisely what customers seek before the appetite surfaces. Here, strategic stocking transforms from intuitive postulation to data-driven precision.

Enhancing Decision-Making Agility

Harnessing the power of real-time analytics and predictive modeling elevates decision-making from reactionary to anticipatory. It imbues organizations with cognitive agility, equipping them to conduct dynamic 'what-if' analysis, where multitudinous scenarios are evaluated before actions coalesce into execution.

In logistics, for instance, companies deploy digital twins to visualize supply chain networks, analyzing real-time conditions such as weather, transportation delays, and geopolitical shifts. Predictive modeling then simulates various disruptions or opportunities, allowing logistics managers to allocate resources, reconfigure routes, and adapt seamlessly, maintaining delivery timelines and cost efficiencies.

Caution and Considerations

Real-time analytics and predictive modeling, despite their sophistication, demand scrupulous calibration and continual refinement.   Models hinge upon data quality and predictive validity, relying on each dataset's timeliness and veracity.   Organizations must ensure that underlying algorithms are free from biases and encapsulated with transparency—a vigilant practice against the specter of inferential error.

Moreover, regulatory compliance introduces its own intricacies.   Particularly in sectors like healthcare or finance, where stakeholder trust is paramount, adhering to data privacy guidelines is non-negotiable, necessitating robust security measures and ethical standards to sustain moral accountability.

Transformative Narratives: Real-World Applications

The power of real-time analytics and predictive modeling branches expansively across industry sectors. In aeronautics, digital twins of jet engines fuse these methodologies to optimize fuel efficiency and predict maintenance turnaround, empowered through a digital representation at cruising altitudes.

In education, digital twins model individualized learning pathways, leveraging real-time performance metrics and predictive trends to customize pedagogical approaches, enhancing student engagement, and improving outcomes—a vivid demonstration of tailoring insights to educational aspirations.

In the awe-inspiring panorama of digital twin

functionality, real-time analytics and predictive modeling craft an interpretative space where insights are not merely gleaned but actively constructed and acted upon. Their integrative wit transforms unyielding complexity into attainable clarity, charting categories of foresight where ambiguity once reigned.

Thus, when digital twins merge dynamic analytics with strategic prediction, they shed light on transformative pathways, igniting a journey toward a horizon throbbing with potential. As tools of empowerment, they become architects of a future-leaning attitude—a timeless catalyst residing at the crossroads of innovation, intelligence, and endless horizons of exploration.

6.5 Ensuring Data Quality and Security

In the realm where digital twins operate, data serves as both the foundation and the framework. It is the raw material from which virtual replicas of physical systems are built, animated, and refined. But not all data is created equal. Beyond the quantity, the quality of data and its security are paramount—ensuring that insights drawn from digital twins are not only accurate but also protected against external threats. This is a narrative of vigilance, where ensuring data quality and security is akin to holding a double-edged sword, each sharp edge representing opportunities and challenges that need deft handling.

Data Quality: The Cadence of Precision

The cornerstone of any digital twin's effectiveness lies in the integrity and fidelity of the data it processes. High-quality data ensures reliability, veracity, and insightfulness, lending itself to accurate simulations and analyses.

However, the path to maintaining data quality is riddled with complexities, requiring a meticulous approach to cleansing, validation, and consistency—transformative efforts that echo the fastidiousness of ancient alchemists seeking to turn base metals into gold.

The Five Pillars of Data Quality

To truly harness the power of digital twins, organizations must cater to the five pillars that define data quality:

- **Accuracy**: The data must accurately represent the real-world scenarios it is meant to emulate. A digital twin of a manufacturing line, for instance, needs precise data on machinery operations and performance conditions to provide credible simulations.

- **Completeness**: Incomplete datasets can lead to flawed or partial insights. Ensuring comprehensive data capture means capturing a full spectrum of relevant variables, akin to a painter ensuring every corner of a canvas is adorned with color.

- **Consistency**: Data must be consistently formatted and verified to avoid discrepancies, especially when sourced from multiple channels. An errant decimal point or misalignment could send simulations skewing wildly off course.

- **Timeliness**: The velocity of data—its promptness and frequency—impacts how well a digital twin reflects current realities. In real-time analytics, latency can erode relevancy, much like stale newsprint sullies topicality.

- **Validity**: Data should conform to a standardized format or predefined rulesets, ensuring that information adheres to requirements and expectations necessary for meaningful interpretation.

144

Case Study: Healthcare Data Quality

In healthcare, where data quality can directly impact patient outcomes, rigorous protocols are enacted to safeguard accuracy and completeness. Electronic health records, IoT-enabled monitors, and diagnostic tools generate oceans of data, demanding an interconnected approach to cleaning, validating, and standardizing datasets.

Consider a digital twin representing a patient's cardiovascular system tailored for cardiologists to implement personalized treatment plans. Here, accuracy is non-negotiable, as misrepresentative data could influence medication dosages, potentially leading to adverse consequences. Thus, healthcare professionals rely extensively on data stewardship programs and validation layers to ensure quality.

Data Security: The Shield of Trust

While quality elevates data, security safeguards it. Protecting data is fundamental to maintaining trust, ensuring that the vast streams of information feeding digital twins remain immune to breaches, manipulations, or theft. The measures enacted here are equivalent to securing a citadel against invaders—a fortress of protocols and practices designed to thwart unauthorized access.

A Historical Context of Secrets and Security

The importance of securing information traces back to antiquity, from the coded messages of Roman times to the cryptographic endeavors of World War II. Each era recognized the power of information and the necessity to protect it, evolving strategies to counteract espionage and subterfuge.

Fast forward to the digital age and the vast amounts of

data whizzing through networks command an equally robust safeguarding effort. With digital twins, the challenge escalates, given the sensitivity and real-time nature of the data involved. Cybersecurity meshes with data quality objectives, together forming a fabric of resilience.

Strategies for Robust Data Security

A comprehensive security posture encompasses:

- **Encryption**: Data is encrypted both at rest and during transmission, rendering it unreadable to unauthorized parties. This ensures that even if intercepted, raw data remains indecipherable—a modern cloak of invisibility.

- **Access Control**: Strict access controls determine who can view or manipulate data, governed by authentication processes and user permissions—analogous to guarding a sacred library where only vetted scholars may enter.

- **Monitoring and Detection**: Proactive monitoring tools surveil data flows for anomalies, potential breaches, or irregularities, prompting swift remedial actions before vulnerabilities are exploited.

- **Regular Audits**: Conducting regular security audits and penetration testing ensures that defenses remain robust and adaptive to emerging threats.

- **Compliance**: Adherence to data protection regulations, such as GDPR or CCPA, assures compliance, emphasizing transparency and fortifying user trust.

Application in the Financial Sector

In finance, where digital twins simulate financial systems or analyze transaction data to forecast market trends, stringent security protocols must neutralize risks associated with cyber threats. Organizations invest heavily in secure communication channels, data encryption, and multi-factor authentication to preserve the sanctity of financial data environments.

Within this sector, the integrity of data translates directly into organizational reputation, making security a boardroom priority, converging business practices with technological vigilance.

As data flows grow more complex, intertwined with digital twins driving decision-making and innovation, a proactive commitment to both quality and security becomes imperative. Building organizational cultures that prioritize data management disciplines from the ground up is fundamental to this success.

Adopting systems with real-time data quality monitoring, automated validation routines, and robust security layers helps ensure that digital twins continue to offer transformative potential without compromise—safeguarding the purity of insights they provide.

Ultimately, in this synergy of assurance and foresight, digital twins transcend mere technological artifacts to become stewards of tomorrow's knowledge—a digital awakening supported by the bedrock tandems of data quality and security. This convergence crafts a matrix of possibilities, instructive yet prudent, in a world where insights remain unerring and uplifting, sheltered in the embrace of secure stewardship and illuminated by the luminescence of quality-driven analytics.

Chapter 7

Digital Twins and the Internet of Things (IoT)

The Internet of Things (IoT) significantly enhances digital twin capabilities by providing constant, real-time data streams from physical devices. IoT devices facilitate tighter integration and connectivity, enabling more precise simulations and analyses. This synergy allows for improved real-time monitoring, efficient predictive maintenance, and optimized system operations. However, integrating IoT with digital twins also presents challenges in data management, interoperability, and security. This chapter examines the pivotal role of IoT in expanding the functionality and applicability of digital twins, addressing both opportunities and associated challenges.

7.1 IoT Devices and Connectivity

To understand the reciprocal dance between digital twins and the Internet of Things (IoT), one must first appreciate the IoT's pivotal role as the whisperer of the analog world—transforming tangible entities into inexhaustible fonts of digital insight. Fundamentally, IoT devices enable connectivity and continuous data flow, a process threading the world's dynamic heartbeats into the structured fabric of digital twins.

The Dawn of Connectivity: A Journey Through Time

The evolution of interconnectedness is a saga reaching back to the advent of electric telegraphy, which first bridged distances with dots and dashes over a century ago. As humans mastered communication technologies, we became ever-more adept at knitting earthly operations into digital expanses.

However, it was not until the conceptualization of IoT in the late 20th century that the notion of a truly interconnected world took hold. Kevin Ashton, who coined the term around 1999, envisaged a new dawn where everyday objects communicated through the internet, foreshadowing today's reality where data from 'smart' devices feeds intelligent systems.

The proliferation of IoT devices exemplifies this vision, where embedded sensors sense, collect, and transmit information on everything from ambient conditions to operational performance. This interconnected lattice underpins today's digital landscape, providing a seamless interface that bridges the gap between the physical and digital realms.

The Role of IoT Devices: Connecting the Dots

Imagine a symphony orchestra where each musician plays a specific instrument, contributing to a harmonious rendition when guided by the conductor. IoT devices are the musicians in the grand symphony of digital twins, each contributing essential pieces of data that, when interwoven, create a comprehensive representation of reality.

- **Sensor Networks**: IoT devices equipped with sensors capture a vast array of environmental and operational data—temperature, humidity, speed, and pressure—all of which serve as the lifeblood of digital twins. These sensors feed detailed observations to digital twins, constructing dynamic representations that evolve with real-time conditions.

- **Connectivity Protocols**: Enabling a seamless flow of information, connectivity protocols like Wi-Fi, Bluetooth, and cellular networks secure the passage of data between IoT devices and centralized analytics platforms. This connectivity is crucial for real-time data transmission, enabling digital twins to provide up-to-the-second clarity on the systems they model.

- **Edge Computing**: Enhanced by IoT, edge computing processes data close to the source, enabling rapid analytics and decision-making at the data's point of origin. By reducing latency, this setup amplifies the responsiveness of digital twins, furnishing rapid-fire insights needed for immediate action.

Practical Applications: IoT in Action

The impact of IoT on digital twins transcends theoretical construct, weaving impressive narratives across industries.

- **Smart Cities**: IoT devices form the backbone of smart cities, where networked sensors monitor traffic flows, energy consumption, and public safety. These devices funnel data into digital twins, which model urban systems, offering insights into optimizing municipal services, reducing congestion, and improving water management.

- **Industrial Monitoring**:   In manufacturing, IoT devices collect data across production lines, monitoring equipment health, and performance metrics.   Digital twins of these industrial systems predict maintenance needs and refine industrial processes,   driving operational efficiency and reducing downtime.

- **Healthcare Innovations**:   Wearable IoT devices capture continuous health metrics—heart rates, glucose levels, sleep patterns—integrating this data into patient-specific digital twins.   These twins allow clinicians to track health over time, personalize treatment plans, and predict potential health issues before they escalate.

Interconnected Challenges: The Path to Seamless Integration

Although the contributions of IoT devices to digital twins are immense, the process of integration is not devoid of challenges.   Varied standards, devices, and manufacturers converge upon systems,   requiring interoperability and coordinated infrastructure.

Efforts to enhance compatibility encompass developing universal communication protocols and employing middleware solutions capable of translating between assorted ecosystems. This 'common language' facilitates a harmonious integration across diverse IoT devices, enriching the digital twin narrative.

Moreover, as data travels across networked devices, establishing robust cybersecurity measures is paramount. Protecting data from unauthorized access and breaches demands encryption, secure channels, and stringent authentication protocols—a necessary endeavor to maintain trust and reliability in IoT interactions.

Success Stories: Navigating the IoT Frontier

Industry trailblazers demonstrate the prowess of IoT devices in augmenting digital twin efficacy.

- **Rolls-Royce**: Renowned for its jet engines, Rolls-Royce integrates IoT devices into engine components, generating real-time performance data. These insights funnel into digital twins, predicting maintenance needs, improving fuel efficiency, and optimizing operational capabilities—inventerizing a near-archetypal example of inter-industry synergy.

- **Bosch**: The multinational engineering company employs IoT sensors within its factories to create digital twins of manufacturing processes. These twins allow Bosch to predict equipment failures, reduce energy consumption, and improve product quality, encapsulating the transformative potential of IoT in driving smart manufacturing.

The IoT-Digital Twin Horizon: A Promising Future

As IoT devices proliferate, the connectivity they offer achieves new heights, bringing complementary technologies such as machine learning and augmented reality into the fold. These collaborations open new horizons for enhanced functionalities and coordination—establishing a backbone for the sophisticated operations of autonomous systems, predictive analytics, and beyond.

Envision autonomous vehicles, emboldened by IoT connectivity, ciphering data from infrastructure sensors and weather stations, merging them into digital twins for enhanced navigation—a digital symphony deftly orchestrating mobility with precision.

The confluence of IoT devices and digital twins paints a vivid tableau where data connectivity flourishes, crossing traditional boundaries to foster understanding and innovation. Together, they elevate each industry's potential, continuously weaving a networked tapestry that makes the invisible visible, the complex manageable, and the future advantageously navigable.

Through seamless connectivity, IoT devices endow digital twins with life-like responsiveness, creating a landscape rich with insights ready to be harnessed in inventive, impactful, and inspiring ways. As we create, simulate, and innovate within this harmonious sphere, we approach a world that is smarter, more efficient, and undeniably connected—a world where the tangible and intangible unite with boundless possibility.

7.2 Integration with Digital Twins

The marriage of the physical and digital realms through digital twins represents one of the most profound technological unifications of our time. This synergy provides a mirror that reflects, anticipates, and optimizes the very systems it models. At the heart of this innovation is integration—the seamless weaving together of diverse technologies, data streams, and analytical tools into a coherent, and dynamic tapestry.

Historical Context: From Isolation to Integration

The path from isolation to integration can be traced back through history. Consider the first steam engines: mechanical marvels functioning in silo. As these machines became more complex, interdependencies emerged—forging an imperative for integration within systems to ensure harmony and efficiency.

Fast forward to the age of computers, and we witness the same imperative. Initially isolated, these machines soon transformed into networked nodes through the invention of the internet, enabling communication and coordination on an unprecedented scale. Similarly, today's digital twins demand the integration of a multitude of inputs—sensors, algorithms, and human insights—melding them into unified, intelligent entities.

Digital Transformation: The Fabric of Integration

Integration within digital twins represents an intricate dance of digital transformation, where multiple threads are woven into a seamless whole. At its core, this integration involves harmonizing varied technologies, from IoT devices and cloud platforms to real-time analytics and AI, facilitating a level of interaction that was previously unattainable.

Consider the example of modern supply chains. Here, digital twins are employed as virtual replicas of logistics networks, integrating data from fleets of vehicles, warehouse inventories, and customer orders. This enables real-time visibility and responsiveness, allowing businesses to optimize routes, reduce costs, and enhance service delivery—all while minimizing the carbon footprint.

The integration extends beyond conventional systems into emerging domains, such as augmented reality (AR). In manufacturing, for instance, AR can be integrated with digital twins to provide real-time, overlayed visual guidance on assembly lines, assisting workers by highlighting procedural steps and alerting them to potential issues—enhancing accuracy and efficiency.

Facilitating Continuous Feedback

A central hallmark of integration with digital twins is

the establishment of continuous feedback loops. These loops carry real-time data from physical systems to their virtual counterparts, allowing them to perceive and predict the states of the systems they represent.

Take, for instance, the automotive industry, where digital twins integrate feedback from IoT sensors in vehicles, simulating the impact of driving conditions on engine efficiency.   These insights are relayed to manufacturers, enhancing vehicle designs and improving fuel consumption—a proactive approach that replaces guesswork with data-driven refinement.

Consider healthcare innovations, where digital twins utilized by clinicians are tethered to patient data from wearable devices. This integration enables a continuous flow of biometric data, facilitating the real-time monitoring of patients' vitals. Doctors can make informed decisions on treatment interventions, providing dynamically updated care paths customized for individual needs.

Practical Applications Across Industries

The act of integration breeds creativity.   Across industries, digital twins are reimagining operational landscapes, offering distinct advantages:

- **Aviation**: Airlines use digital twins to integrate data from aircraft sensors, maintenance logs, and flight records.   This comprehensive insight ensures aircraft safety, reduces downtime, and streamlines route planning—all critical to operational efficiency in an industry that never sleeps.

- **Energy Management**: Power utilities employ digital twins to integrate smart grid data with weather forecasts and energy demand analytics. This enables them to anticipate fluctuations in energy supply and demand, optimizing grid performance and facilitating the incorporation of renewable energy sources.

- **Retail**: In retail, digital twins merge transactional data with supply chain metrics, allowing businesses to tailor inventory strategies, speed up delivery processes, and create personalized customer experiences. This integration ensures a fluid, responsive retail environment that adapts to shifting consumer demands.

Challenges in Integration: Navigating an Evolving Landscape

Despite the manifold opportunities, integrating digital twins introduces its own set of challenges. Primary among them is ensuring interoperability among diverse technologies and data sources. The imagined symphony of collaboration can falter if the instruments themselves refuse to play in tune with the same score.

Overcoming proprietary constraints and bridging disparate systems requires adopting standardized protocols and interoperable solutions. Additionally, balancing the trade-off between extensibility and complexity is critical—making certain that integrations are scalable while maintaining simplicity and manageability.

There is also the unignorable challenge of data privacy and security, necessitating stringent protective measures to safeguard sensitive information exchanged within digital twin environments. Establishing robust cybersecurity frameworks, coupled with ethical guidelines, ensures stakeholder trust and the integrity of the integrated system.

The Human Element: A Collaborative Dance

157

While technology drives integration, the human element remains paramount. Fostering cross-disciplinary collaboration among engineers, data scientists, and domain experts is essential, ensuring that the integration pathways reflect both technical prowess and domain-specific wisdom.

Training and change management initiatives help organizations cultivate a culture of integration, encouraging personnel to embrace digital twins and the augmented capabilities they offer. This harmonious collaboration ensures that the human touch enriches the digital tapestry, amplifying the innovation woven into each system.

A Vision for the Future

As digital twins continue to mature, the integration with emerging technologies and insights will only deepen. The convergence of AI, IoT, and quantum computing heralds an era where digital twins will not only replicate but actively co-manage and co-create realities, forging unprecedented pathways of innovation and efficiency.

Imagine the promise of smart cities whose services— transportation, energy, waste management—operate seamlessly through integrated digital twins, delivering efficiency, sustainability, and harmony to urban dwellers. Such a future invites us all to engage and redefine the possibilities for our societies in thoughtful and meaningful ways.

As digital twins continue to mature, the integration with emerging technologies and insights will only deepen. The convergence of AI, IoT, and quantum computing heralds an era where digital twins will not only replicate but actively co-manage and co-create realities, forging unprecedented pathways of innovation and efficiency.

Imagine the promise of smart cities whose services—transportation, energy, waste management—operate seamlessly through integrated digital twins, delivering efficiency, sustainability, and harmony to urban dwellers. Such a future invites us all to engage and redefine the possibilities for our societies in thoughtful and meaningful ways.

7.3 Enhancing Real-Time Monitoring

In the digital age, the distinction between minutes and moments can mean the difference between success and setback. As industries grapple with ever-faster rates of change, the ability to monitor systems in real-time evolves from luxury to necessity. Digital twins, when combined with real-time monitoring, offer an exquisite capability: transforming raw data into immediate insights, enabling swift interventions and fostering an agile approach to operations.

A Historical Glance at Monitoring: From Dials to Dashboards

Monitoring is not a novel concept. It has been a staple of human ingenuity—an inherent necessity dating back to ancient foresters who monitored weather to protect their crops, or astronomers who traced celestial movements with patient precision. The industrial era upped the ante as steam engines required constant vigilance; boiler pressures were monitored via iron dials, with engineers ready to act at the first twitch of the needle.

With the advent of the computer age, these efforts transformed into dashboards displaying vital statistics of machinery and processes. Yet, the paradigm shift truly came with real-time capabilities, merging live data streams with adaptive control systems. Digital twins amplify this concept, offering a dashboard that doesn't just display but also analyzes, predicts, and adapts.

Real-Time Monitoring Defined: Alive and Immediate

At its core, real-time monitoring involves the continuous tracking of data, a perpetual pulse-taking of systems, which offers an immediate picture of operational status. It's akin to a live news feed, delivering up-to-the-second information directly from the source. Digital twins, functioning as sophisticated virtual observers, enable this through integrated sensor networks and seamless data streams.

Consider a hydroelectric plant where real-time monitoring mechanisms use digital twins to track water flow, equipment status, and electricity output. Any anomaly—a surge in water levels or a sudden drop in efficiency—triggers alerts, sparking preemptive adjustments. This ability to pivot swiftly ensures resources are conserved and potential damages are averted, underscoring the power of an ever-vigilant system.

Industries Unleashed: Applications Across Sectors

The magic of real-time monitoring is its omnipresence across sectors—an efficiency enhancer in manufacturing, a safeguard in healthcare, and an optimizer in logistics.

- **Manufacturing**: Real-time monitoring in manufacturing harnesses digital twins to scrutinize production lines for inefficiencies. By collecting and analyzing data on machinery performance and product quality, digital twins offer actionable insights into system health, reducing downtimes and enhancing throughput— effectively making micro-edits in the ongoing storyline of production.

- **Healthcare**: In the medical sphere, real-time monitoring revolutionizes patient care. Wearable devices track biometrics such as heart rate, blood glucose levels, or oxygen saturation. When funneled into patient-specific digital twins, doctors receive real-time health snapshots, allowing precise interventions and optimizations in treatment regimens—a dance of metrics that enhances patient outcomes.

- **Logistics**: For logistics, real-time monitoring means mastering motion. Transport vehicles equipped with IoT devices feed live data into digital twins, which map routes, predict delays, and optimize deliveries all while managing fuel efficiency. This real-time orchestration ensures packages arrive swiftly and intact, enhancing customer satisfaction and minimizing costs.

Supporting Scalability and Flexibility

Incorporating real-time monitoring requires robust infrastructures that support the continuously evolving data flows digital twins demand. This often involves scaling existing IT frameworks to process and analyze high-frequency updates promptly, a capability supported by distributed computing and edge technologies.

Edge computing, for instance, processes data at the periphery of the network—close to where it's generated, reducing latency and freeing up bandwidth for essential analytics. Consider autonomous vehicles using digital twins that rely on edge computing to make split-second navigation decisions—each adjustment informed by live inputs processed locally for maximal agility.

Transforming Data into Action: Predictive Feedback

The synergy between real-time monitoring and digital twins extends beyond observation to intelligence. Predictive feedback systems use data from digital twins to preemptively signal potential issues—predictive maintenance being a signature application.

In aviation, digital twins monitoring engines predict wear and tear parameters, scheduling maintenance before minor discrepancies manifest into malfunctions. These prescient alerts lessen disruptions and ensure that fleets remain airworthy, balancing operational efficiency with passenger safety.

Navigating Challenges: The Road to Real-Time Adoption

Despite its transformative capabilities, real-time monitoring is not without challenges. Handling vast data volumes in real-time can stress existing networks, necessitating investments in scalable infrastructure and data processing capabilities. Organizations also must navigate the complexities of selecting appropriate metrics—distinguishing signal from noise to ensure clarity and focus.

Moreover, ensuring data accuracy, security, and privacy in real-time environments is paramount. Protecting sensitive information in healthcare or finance calls for fortified cybersecurity measures and compliant data governance frameworks, accommodating the tempo of real-time operations while safeguarding trust.

Interoperability and Standardization: A Necessary Symphony

Interoperability presents another layer of complexity. With diverse legacy systems and modern technologies converging in real-time frameworks, harmonizing data standards and interfaces is essential. Industry leaders are responding through standardized protocols and open-source initiatives, promoting universal compatibility and reducing silos—a collaborative symphony composing the sheet music of real-time integration.

The Human Element: Augmenting Expertise

While the technological marvel of real-time monitoring unfolds, the human element remains indispensable. These systems amplify human expertise, equipping professionals with nuanced, data-driven perspectives. Empowered with real-time insights, decision-makers can exercise informed judgment, balancing analytical intelligence with experiential wisdom.

In crafting the systems that govern our future, interdisciplinary teams—engineers, data specialists, and domain experts—must collaborate to sculpt interfaces and analytics that translate data into accessible, actionable intuitions reflective of organizational goals.

Imagining Futures: The Real-Time Frontier

As we stand on the cusp of ever-more integrative real-time environments, digital twins remain pivotal in redefining operational landscapes. Emerging technologies, like artificial intelligence and machine learning, will foster evolving analytics—a commitment to endless improvement, deepening insights, and ever-greater adaptability.

Looking forward, envision the collective intelligence of smart cities—digital twins tirelessly monitoring public infrastructure, utilities, and transportation networks autonomously adjusting city operations, maximizing resource efficiency, and aiding swift crisis responses.

Real-time monitoring through digital twins is a node of transformation—bridging the ephemeral visibility of systems with the suppleness of informed intervention. By harnessing the intrinsic value of immediacy, it captures moments and molds them into opportunities, crafting a future where responsiveness isn't just possible—it's intrinsic.

This real-time renaissance reshapes how we comprehend, interact, and optimize the world around us. As it evolves, we witness a symbiosis that equips industries with dynamism and precision, inviting mankind to experience an era defined by clarity and connectivity, channeling the immediacy of now into meaningful, measurable progress.

7.4 Improving Predictive Maintenance

Imagine a world where machines speak their own future—where engines whisper of emergent fatigue before grinding to a halt, transformers murmur maintenance needs long before any spark of failure. This is not the speculative wonder of science fiction but the tangible reality of predictive maintenance, an innovative approach that synergizes with digital twins to transform the very essence of operation and upkeep.

From Reactive to Predictive: A Paradigm Shift

For much of industrial history, maintenance has been reactive, bound by the inevitability of wear and breakdown. The blacksmith replaced a shattered wheel after it splintered under pressure; engineers restored systems only when halted by unscheduled breakdowns. Over time, preventive maintenance matured as a conceptual framework, bringing scheduled service and routine check-ups, much like preventive care in medicine, to mitigate risk and extend equipment life.

Yet, a revolutionary evolution arose alongside

digital transformation: predictive maintenance—a methodology designed not only to maintain but to preempt. Here, digital twins play a central role, coupling sensor-derived data with advanced analytics to anticipate and address issues in advance of their manifest decline.

How Predictive Maintenance Works: The Knit of Data and Insight

At its heart, predictive maintenance weaves together data, analytics, and modeling to construct a rich tapestry of insight. It draws upon signals from IoT-enabled sensors embedded within systems, feeding real-time information about performance, environmental factors, and usage into digital twins. These digital replicas act as vigilant prognosticators, continuously modeling scenarios and predicting potential failure points.

This approach lessens reliance on fixed schedules, allowing maintenance activities to be executed on an as-needed basis—a choreography shaped by condition-based assessments rather than fixed calendars. Consider the whispering heart of a factory's machinery: as values cross predefined thresholds or reveal anomalous trends, alerts spark, calling for preemptive action and avoiding excessive wear or critical failures.

Historical Context: From Time-Based to Condition-Based Maintenance

The roots of predictive maintenance draw from foundations laid during the mid-20th century. As industries expanded post-World War II, the need for durable and reliable operations grew, spurring research into time-based maintenance (TBM)—a strategy prescribing routine maintenance based on the calendar or usage frequency. TBM seemed a logical simplification but, inevitably, led to functional inefficiencies and unnecessary disruptions.

However, with the advent of computers and remote monitoring technology, condition-based maintenance (CBM) emerged, leveraging real-time diagnostics to assess equipment health and inform timely interventions. Predictive maintenance takes CBM further, incorporating machine learning and statistical models to offer foresight—a move that subtly transforms the role of maintenance from necessity to innovation.

Sectoral Applications: Real-World Transformations

- **Aerospace**: In a realm where reliability transcends preference to become imperative, aircraft turbines embody predictive maintenance's excellence. Sensors record fine-grained metrics related to vibration, temperature, and engine thrust, transmitting data to digital twins. Predictive models analyze this information to forecast service windows—allowing airlines like Delta or Boeing to plan ahead, minimizing grounded time and maximizing fleet availability.

- **Manufacturing**: One of the prime beneficiaries, the manufacturing sector, exults in predictive maintenance's promise. Ensconcing IoT devices within robotic arms and conveyor belts transforms production lines into intelligent networks. By modeling machine health, digital twins identify issues before they cascade into assembly line pauses, sustaining a rhythm that marries produc-tivity with foresight—a ballet uninterrupted by abrupt intermissions.

- **Energy and Utilities**: In energy grids, where continuity underpins both livelihoods and economies, predictive maintenance ensures both network health and customer satisfaction. Critical substations and transformers are monitored, with digital twins predicting and diagnosing faults before outages occur, enabling seamless transitions to backup systems. This approach affirms stability, preserving unyielding power flows to urban centers and rural outposts alike.

Technological Synergies and Innovation

The profound impact of predictive maintenance is amplified through advanced analytics, AI, and machine learning. Machine learning algorithms offer predictive maintenance its most compelling voice—capable of identifying and interpreting subtle, non-linear patterns across datasets too vast for traditional methods.

Artificial intelligence enables adaptive learning models, updating digital twins as they ingest fresh data streams, honing predictive accuracy and extending their interpretative reach over time. This continuous cycle of learning reflects a cascading improvement that delivers heightened confidence and optimized operations.

The integration of edge computing further enriches predictive maintenance by processing data close to its source, allowing prompt decision-making unaffected by latency—an embodiment of agility and immediacy central to any maintenance philosophy.

Challenges and Considerations

Even as there is much to be lauded, the road to predictive maintenance isn't without challenges. The complexity of integrating systems across heterogeneous environments demands robust interoperability frameworks and data standards. Sufficient training to crack the code of these integrated systems is essential, as workforce readiness evolves hand in hand with technological insights.

Furthermore, just like with other predictive technologies, the specter of false positives and negatives looms; thus, accuracy is fundamental, necessitating continuous model validation, calibration, and improvement—a form of qualitative oversight overseeing quantitative realms.

Security, too, acts as a threshold concern. As machines telegraph intimate operational data, securing both data integrity and privacy becomes imperative—fortifying the digital ecosystem with the vigilance akin to a well-guarded treasure trove.

The Road Ahead: An Integrated Future of Predictive Potential

Looking forward, the synthesis of digital twins with IoT and analytics will see predictive maintenance extend its reach beyond machinery into new frontiers, crafting intelligent infrastructures that autonomously refine their operational parameters. As these capabilities unfold, they will form the backbone of smart cities, autonomous vehicles, and even personalized home systems—ushering in an era of sustained optimization without human intervention.

A Transformative Outlook

Predictive maintenance, augmented by digital twins, exemplifies how contemporary technology unites past expertise with future potential. It strips away inefficiencies that once rendered machinery vulnerable, replacing uncertainty with calculated assurance.

In sum, predictive maintenance offers not just a glimpse into the mechanical ether of time but a reassurance that the tomorrows of industry are informed by the betterment of today—a commitment to continuity in progress validated by the art and science of measurable foresight.

7.5 Challenges and Limitations

Digital twins and the Internet of Things (IoT) have carved a path of incredible potential and transformative influence. Yet, as with any technological innovation, they also walk hand-in-hand with a myriad of challenges and limitations. These range from technical and infrastructural hurdles to ethical and financial concerns, demanding an astute navigation of complexities woven into the fabric of this burgeoning digital landscape.

The Historical Dance of Challenge and Progress

Throughout history, grand technological revolutions have rarely unfolded without accompanying strife. The steam engine may have ushered in the Industrial Revolution, yet its initial designs grappled with inefficiency and safety issues. Likewise, the thrill of the Information Age emerged alongside concerns over digital privacy and security.

Today, as digital twins entwine with IoT, they inherit this paradox of progress—a dualism where staggering potential intersects with real-world impediments.

Data Management and Overload

A primary challenge in the realm of digital twins lies in data management. Given the sheer volume of data flowing from the vast ecosystem of interconnected devices, managing these torrents in a coherent, efficient manner remains formidable. Organizations must wrestle with how to capture, store, and process vast amounts of data without compromising integrity or usability.

The task is akin to being served at a royal feast—you can hardly savor the delicacies if they are all delivered simultaneously. Thus, advanced data management strategies become crucial, calling for investment in scalable

169

cloud solutions, robust database systems, and intelligent analytics tools that can distill meaningful insights from within the deluge.

Moreover, data accessibility poses a challenge of its own. Ensuring that relevant stakeholders have timely access to critical data, while maintaining a balance between privacy and transparency, requires agile systems that can adapt to shifting demands and regulatory requirements.

Interoperability and Integration Complexities

Digital twins and IoT systems thrive on integration, yet achieving a seamless interface among disparate systems is no small feat. Interoperability challenges arise from varying protocols, platforms, and technologies—each vying for its place within the connected tapestry.

This lack of standardization can hinder the smooth flow of data and limit the cohesive functioning of interconnected systems. As companies deploy digital twins across global networks, the complexity of integrated systems increases exponentially, making the orchestration of these digital symphonies challenging, to say the least.

Consider the manufacturing sector, where integrating legacy systems with modern IoT infrastructure demands extensive customization and collaboration, often resulting in delays and increased costs. The solution pivots on industry-wide adoption of open standards and frameworks that facilitate interconnectivity and bridge the divide between old and new.

Security Concerns: The Continual Guardian

Security represents both a challenge and a critical necessity in the digital twin ecosystem. As IoT devices proliferate across industries, they expand the attack surface for potential cybersecurity threats. Ensuring data integrity and protecting against unauthorized access becomes paramount.

Imagine a smart city, teeming with sensors and IoT devices, vulnerable to malicious attacks that could disrupt traffic systems or compromise public safety. Safeguarding these environments requires robust encryption protocols, secure authentication processes, and continuous monitoring to detect and neutralize potential threats.

Moreover, the complexity of these security measures can pose limitations, as organizations must balance robust protection with performance and operational efficiency. It requires a vigilant approach, embedding security into the very architecture of digital systems from inception.

The Weight of Ethical and Privacy Considerations

As digital twins and IoT systems delve into sensitive domains, ethical considerations and privacy concerns arise with heightened significance. The ability of these systems to aggregate intimate data invites scrutiny over how data is collected, utilized, and shared.

Ethical considerations also extend to the potential bias in the algorithms and analytics employed within digital twins, potentially leading to skewed insights and interpretations. Ensuring fairness and neutrality in AI-driven decision-making processes becomes crucial in preventing discriminatory outcomes and reinforcing equitable practices.

Establishing clear ethical guidelines and adherence to regulatory frameworks such as GDPR demonstrates an organizational commitment to trust and accountability, fostering environments where innovation coexists with ethical stewardship.

Financial and Skill-Based Constraints

While the allure of digital twins is compelling, the financial investment required for their adoption can be formidable, particularly for small and medium enterprises. These costs encompass not only the initial deployment but also ongoing maintenance, training, and upgrades.

Furthermore, developing the skills necessary to leverage digital twins presents another constraint, as organizations must cultivate a workforce equipped with the requisite expertise—spanning data analytics, system integration, and domain-specific knowledge. Bridging this skill gap involves strategic investments in education, professional development, and cross-disciplinary collaboration.

Partnerships between academia and industry play a pivotal role in nurturing the talent pipeline, ensuring a workforce ready to harness the potential of digital twins and IoT systems effectively.

Future Directions: Navigating the Path Ahead

Addressing the challenges and limitations of digital twins and IoT requires a concerted effort, fueled by collaboration, innovation, and foresight. By prioritizing open standards, bolstering cybersecurity measures, and embracing ethical practices, organizations can cultivate an ecosystem conducive to growth and innovation.

Collaboration across sectors and geographies serves as the linchpin, fostering an atmosphere of shared progress and open dialogue. It means striving toward solutions that dismantle silos, enhance interoperability, and promote inclusivity.

As we stand poised on the brink of expansive possibility, the narrative of digital twins and IoT reveals itself not just as one of technology, but of humanity—a journey toward a future where challenges are greeted not with reluctance, but with resolve, ensuring these innovations serve the manifold interests of society at large.

In the end, while challenges and limitations accompany the digital twin revolution, they are but stepping stones on the broader journey of technological evolution. As we traverse this landscape, the human element remains steadfast, guiding the intersection of innovation and pragmatism.

Through perseverance, collaboration, and an unwavering commitment to ethical stewardship, we unlock the potential embedded within digital twins—navigating challenges with the insight necessary to shape transformative futures. With each stride, we acknowledge that technology's finest achievements are a testament not only to innovation but to our collective ability to meet challenges with creativity and compassion—ensuring a future that reflects the very best of what it means to be human.

Chapter 8

Future Trends in Digital Twin Technology

Digital twin technology is poised to evolve with advances in artificial intelligence, bolstering analytical capabilities and decision-making precision. Emerging applications across new industries, such as agriculture and education, highlight its expanding relevance. Enhanced interconnectivity and interoperability between systems will become critical, while integration with augmented and virtual reality may offer immersive simulation experiences. The focus on sustainability will drive environmentally friendly uses of digital twins. This chapter explores these future-oriented trends, underscoring the technology's potential to continuously transform industry landscapes and foster innovation.

8.1 Advancements in Artificial Intelligence

Imagine a world where machines not only mimic human intelligence but also amplify it, crafting insights from a sea of data with the precision of a seasoned detective. This is the realm of artificial intelligence (AI), where recent advancements are set to dramatically enhance the capabilities of digital twins—those digital doppelgängers of physical systems—as they forge new paths in processing and analytics.

A Historical Canvas: Shades of Intelligence

To appreciate the dawn of AI's potential, we must traverse its storied past. The tale of AI begins over half a century ago, amidst thinkers who dared to dream of machines capable of learning and reasoning. Early computer scientists, like Alan Turing and John McCarthy, envisioned AI as the next frontier—a noble pursuit to emulate human-like understanding through mechanized logic.

For decades, AI waddled through phases of halcyon promises and wintry AI winters, where progress seemed to stagnate. Yet, each setback fostered resilience, culminating in today's renaissance—a time marked by breakthroughs in machine learning, natural language processing, and computational power.

The Convergence of AI and Digital Twins

In the marriage of AI and digital twins, we find a union where each partner magnifies the strengths of the other. Digital twins offer AI rich environments populated with dynamic datasets, paving the way for AI-driven models to learn, adapt, and optimize systems with unprecedented detail.

As AI algorithms navigate digital twins of manufacturing plants, for instance, they learn patterns of machine behavior—predicting maintenance needs by recognizing subtle deviations in performance metrics. This optimization prolongs equipment lifespan and minimizes downtime, transforming monitoring into foresight.

Machine Learning: The Silent Artisan

Machine learning, an AI subdomain, blossoms within digital twins by absorbing data and refining models based on observed patterns. Imagine algorithms that, like sculptors, chip away at raw data, revealing intricate structures and trends undetectable to the naked eye.

Consider logistics, where AI-driven digital twins analyze traffic data, weather forecasts, and historical delivery records. By learning the ebb and flow of logistical networks, machine learning models suggest optimal routes, forecast delivery delays, and enhance supply chain flexibility. This emergent intelligence redefines efficiency and responsiveness across transportation sectors.

Natural Language Processing: Conversational Composition

Natural Language Processing (NLP) enables computers to grasp and interpret human language. In the confluence with digital twins, NLP transforms user interactions into intuitive dialogues, allowing stakeholders to query and interpret data effortlessly.

For example, a facilities manager might interact with a building's digital twin through voice commands, inquiring about energy usage or temperature regulation. NLP parses these interactions, delivering timely insights and facilitating proactive adjustments. By simplifying communication, NLP bridges the gap between complex data environments and human understanding.

Deep Learning: The Neural Symbiosis

Deep learning, a powerhouse within AI, capitalizes on neural networks to replicate human thought processes. Within digital twins, deep learning models act as guides, instructing systems to learn from vast data layers and execute decisions with refined precision.

In healthcare, digital twins enhanced by deep learning analyze patient data to simulate treatment outcomes, offering evidence-based guidance to clinicians. These simulations integrate genetic, environmental, and behavioral data, suggesting personalized therapeutic paths that maximize efficacy and patient welfare.

Autonomy and Self-Healing: AI Ascendant

Perhaps one of AI's most exciting prospects within digital twins lies in fostering autonomy—the capacity for systems to adapt and self-regulate without direct human intervention. This capability engenders self-healing systems adept at troubleshooting and resolving issues as they arise.

Imagine smart grids embedded with AI-enhanced digital twins that autonomously manage energy flows, adjusting in response to variable outputs from renewable sources. By anticipating potential overloads or shortages, such systems optimize distribution, ensuring energy stability and sustainability.

The Ethical and Societal Dimensions

As AI empowers digital twins with greater agency, ethical considerations assume newfound significance. The deployment of AI in autonomous systems requires an emphasis on transparency, accountability, and ethical standards to facilitate trust and prevent bias.

Moreover, societies must engage in discussions on the implications of AI-driven automation and potential workforce disruptions. Collaborative efforts across policy-makers, industry leaders, and educators are necessary to prepare for the ethical dilemmas and opportunities AI technologies present.

Case Studies: AI in Action with Digital Twins

- **Smart Cities**: Amsterdam exemplifies AI's transformative impact via digital twins in urban planning. By analyzing pedestrian and traffic data, AI-enhanced twins offer insights into optimizing public transit systems, reducing congestion, and improving air quality—tailoring urban experiences to resonate with environmental and citizen needs.

- **Agriculture**: Deploying AI within digital twins, agriculture reaps the benefits of precision farming. Sensors and drones collect data on soil health, crop conditions, and weather patterns, which AI models then process. These insights guide farmers to optimize irrigation, fertilization, and pest control—nurturing enhanced yields through tailored interventions.

Future Horizons: The AI-Digital Twin Trajectory

As AI continues to evolve, next-generation technologies such as quantum computing and neuromorphic computing promise to further elevate digital twins. Quantum algorithms will process information at lightning speed, augmenting decision-making power and enhancing predictive capabilities. Meanwhile, neuromorphic architectures may enable adaptive learning models that mirror biological efficiencies within digital environments.

In the symbiotic dance of AI and digital twins, we uncover a future textured with astounding possibilities and transformative potential. AI infuses digital twins with intellect, enabling them to learn, adapt, and enhance systems—turning data into knowledge and knowledge into action.

This union not only unlocks new dimensions of analytical precision but also facilitates innovation that streamlines processes, enriches human existence, and addresses challenges spanning health, environment, and society. It is a journey that propels us toward understanding, optimizing, and reimagining the world with unbounded creativity and impeccable acumen—a narrative that continues to unfold with each algorithmic beat and digital echo.

8.2   Expansion Across New Industries

As the crescendo of digitalization sweeps across the globe, the ripple effects of digital twin technology are beginning to resonate beyond the frontiers of traditional sectors such as manufacturing and aerospace. The coming years herald an era where digital twins will find fertile ground in a suite of emerging industries—from agriculture and education to retail—paving new avenues for growth and innovation. This metamorphosis mirrors the journey of electricity, which once powered only lamps but soon became the lifeblood of diverse industries from cinema to computing.

Agriculture: Cultivating Data-Driven Farms

Consider the pastoral scenes of agriculture transformed by digital twins—where fields brim with more than crops; they brim with data. In the age-old practice of farming, digital twins emerge as modern-day stewards, optimizing every facet of cultivation with precision and insight.

- **Precision Agriculture**: Farmers, once guided solely by intuition and experience, now harness digital twins integrated with IoT sensors to monitor soil health, meteorological conditions, and crop growth. By simulating different

180

scenarios, these digital twins inform decisions on irrigation, fertilization, and pest control, enhancing yield quality and conserving resources.

For example, a vineyard might utilize digital twins to track microclimates across its terrain. By modeling the nuanced interplay of sunlight, humidity, and soil composition, vintners can tailor their practices, ensuring each grape achieves its quintessential character—a symbiosis of nature and innovation ripe for the tasting.

- **Aquaculture Innovations**: The seas, too, are fertile with possibility. In aquaculture, digital twins provide virtual models of fish farms, simulating water quality, currents, and fish health. These insights help operators maintain optimal conditions, reduce feed waste, and decrease environmental impacts—a newfound harmony between sustainable practices and ocean bounty.

Education: Bridging Learning and Experience

In the hallowed halls of education, digital twins offer a transformative potential that blurs the boundaries between textbook theory and tangible application.

- **Virtual Laboratories**: Imagine physics classrooms where students conduct experiments not confined by physical constraints. Digital twins create virtual lab environments that replicate real-world phenomena, allowing students to explore complex systems safely and economically. This interactive approach enhances understanding and fosters creativity, nurturing the scientists of tomorrow.

- **Personalized Learning Paths**: Digital twins facilitate personalized education by modeling

181

students' strengths, weaknesses, and learning styles. Educators can use these insights to tailor curriculum paths, ensuring each student experiences an education as unique as their fingerprint—an academic journey illumined by adaptability and engagement.

Universities, embracing this technology, design bespoke virtual campus extensions where learners navigate a rich tapestry of resources and experiences, bridging the geographic and logistical divides that often accompany modern education.

Retail: Crafting Consumer Experiences

As the digital marketplace expands, retail is set to undergo a metamorphosis influenced by digital twins that cater to the nuanced demands of modern consumers.

- **Store Optimization**: Within brick-and-mortar stores, digital twins simulate customer flows, inventory turnover, and space utilization. Retailers can experiment with store layouts and product placements in virtual environments to maximize shopping experiences, enhance foot traffic, and streamline operations—a clever choreography of the marketplace floor.

- **Supply Chain Resilience**: From warehousing to logistics, digital twins map the entire supply chain ecosystem, predicting disruptions, managing inventory levels, and analyzing transportation logistics. This holistic view ensures efficiency, reduces waste, and enhances the delivery accuracy—creating seamless bridges between sourcing, stocking, and selling.

182

Consider online giants implementing digital twins to simulate various supply chain scenarios, forecasting consumer trends, or adapting to unexpected global shifts—an agile response rooted in virtual preparedness and market elasticity.

Public Health: Safeguarding Societal Well-being

In the sphere of public health, digital twins promise to underpin robust systems that anticipate and mitigate societal health challenges.

- **Pandemic Response**: By modeling pathogen spread and containment strategies, digital twins inform public health decisions, optimizing resource allocation and policy measures. Cities and nations deploy these simulations to assess interventions—vaccination campaigns, lockdown policies, or healthcare capacity—adapting plans based on predictive insights and real-time data.

- **Hospital Operations**: Hospitals are complex, dynamic organisms in their own right. Digital twins model patient flow, staffing schedules, and equipment utilization, allowing administrators to maximize efficiency and care quality. These predictive capabilities ensure hospitals remain agile, responsive, and resilient—guarding the public's health with foresight and precision.

Energy and Environment: Harmonizing Progress and Preservation

Beyond traditional utilities, digital twins find applications in environmental stewardship and the pursuit of sustainable energy solutions.

- **Renewable Integration**: Digital twins model renewable energy systems, forecasting production based on weather patterns and optimizing integration with existing grids. They inform decisions on energy storage, distribution, and consumption—ensuring a reliable, sustainable, and balanced energy ecosystem.

- **Environmental Monitoring**: From forests to oceans, digital twins simulate environmental systems, monitoring biodiversity, ecosystem health, and climate impacts. These insights inform conservation efforts, guiding interventions to protect natural resources and mitigate human impact, crafting a balanced dialogue between development and preservation.

The Financial Sector: Navigating Complexity and Risk

Even within the financial markets' unpredictable terrain, digital twins offer a compass.

- **Investment Strategy**: Financial institutions employ digital twins to simulate market behavior, forecast economic trends, and stress-test portfolios. By modeling risk scenarios and investment opportunities, they enhance strategic planning and decision-making—a calculated navigation through volatility.

- **Regulatory Compliance**: Digital twins assist with compliance by modeling regulatory environments and ensuring alignment with complex legal frameworks. This proactive approach reduces risk and promotes transparency, creating trustworthy financial systems—a vigilant custodian of financial integrity.

184

Challenges on the Horizon: Navigating New Territories

As digital twins permeate new industries, they invite both opportunities and challenges. Ensuring data quality remains a foundational necessity, requiring robust infrastructures that support accurate modeling and secure integration. Interoperability across platforms and sectors must be achieved, catalyzing innovation across industries while avoiding technological silos.

Ethical considerations loom large as digital twins engage with sensitive data—from student information to medical records. Transparent practices, ethical guidelines, and robust privacy measures are vital to ensure trust and accountability.

Embracing the Collective Vision

The expansion of digital twins into new industries underscores our collective capacity to harness technology for the betterment of society. This journey invites stakeholders—innovators, policymakers, educators, and citizens alike—to shape a future where digital twins optimize and enrich every sphere of human endeavor.

In embracing this future, digital twins serve not just as practical tools but also as philosophical muses—reminding us to balance progress with purpose and innovation with integrity. In shaping the world of tomorrow, digital twins propel us towards possibilities guided by creativity, insight, and empathy—crafting a landscape of interconnected brilliance that echoes humanity's greatest aspirations.

8.3   Increased Interconnectivity and Interoperability

Step into a world where boundaries blur, and hyperconnectivity reigns supreme—a place where devices and systems converse effortlessly across digital landscapes, driving innovation and efficiency. This vision is powered by the escalating forces of interconnectivity and interoperability, essential elements for digital twins that encourage seamless interaction and unbounded collaboration.

Historical Context: From Isolated Islands to Unified Networks

To appreciate the current wave of connectivity, one must journey back to a time when systems existed in isolation, akin to solitary islands. Each functioned independently, with minimal interaction beyond narrowly defined interfaces—a reality that posed challenges for scalability and integration.

Enter the late 20th century, where computer networking began erasing these divides, laying the groundwork for what we now embrace as the internet—an interconnected web unrestricted by geography. This evolution paved the way for the cooperative ecosystems we witness today, where devices and platforms coexist harmoniously, guided by protocols and standards that ensure their mutual comprehension.

The Confluence of Connectivity and Interoperability

In the domain of digital twins, interconnectivity and interoperability serve as essential pillars holding up an edifice of seamless exchange and analytic symphony. They propel digital twins beyond single-use constructs, inviting multiple systems and participants to synchronize their efforts and amplify collective intelligence.

Interconnectivity: The Digital Linkage

Interconnectivity refers to the capacity for different systems to connect and communicate effectively. Like synapses linking neurons, each connection opens channels for data flow, fostering an expansive network where digital twins and their real-world counterparts engage in continuous dialogue.

Consider the intricate dance of smart homes, where IoT-enabled devices—thermostats, security cameras, lighting systems—coalesce into integrated networks. Data from these sources enter a unified digital twin, offering homeowners intelligent insights into energy usage, security, and automation, be it through mobile devices or central hubs. This connectivity enhances control and comfort, transforming mere residences into ecosystems attuned to their inhabitants.

Interoperability: The Universal Translator

Interoperability transcends connection by ensuring different systems and devices can work in unison, irrespective of manufacturer or platform. It provides a common language for communication, enabling diverse technologies to interpret and utilize data efficiently, thus promoting cooperative engagement and resource optimization.

A robust example can be found in the healthcare sector, where patient data emerges from a myriad of sources—hospital EMRs, wearable tech, lab results. Through interoperability, this diverse data integrates into cohesive digital twin models. These twins offer practitioners a comprehensive view of patient health, facilitating diagnosis and treatment planning, crafting a continuous care narrative that transcends the fragmentary limitations of erstwhile silos.

Real-World Applications: Unleashing Potential

The potential unleashed by increased interconnectivity
and interoperability echoes across myriad industries, igniting powerful transformations and unveiling new dimensions of functionality.

- **Urban Infrastructure**

  Within smart cities, digital twins embody
  interconnected frameworks linking public
  infrastructure, transit systems, energy grids,
  and environmental monitoring.   Enhanced
  interconnectivity ensures data flows seamlessly
  across municipal sectors, allowing city planners
  to optimize traffic flows, resource distribution,
  and emergency responses—rendering urban
  management both efficient and adaptive.

- **Supply Chain Management**

  Global supply chains thrive on synchronized
  operations driven by interoperable systems.
  Digital twins map logistics networks, integrating
  data from suppliers, transporters, and distributors
  in real-time. With actionable insights, enterprises
  streamline inventory management, mitigate
  blockages, and enhance resilience—a sophisticated
  ballet orchestrated through transparency and
  foresight.

- **Environmental Monitoring**

  Interoperable sensors deployed in ecosystems
  capture crucial environmental data—temperature
  fluctuations, pollutant levels, and biodiversity
  metrics—feeding integrated digital twin models.
  Researchers and policymakers leverage these
  insights to assess ecosystem health and inform

conservation strategies—crafting symbiotic solutions that harmonize development with sustainability.

Technical Challenges: Navigating the Labyrinth

Despite its promise, achieving seamless interconnectivity and interoperability comes fraught with challenges that demand resolve and ingenuity.

- **Data Standardization**

  Diverse data origins necessitate uniformity to enable compatibility. Establishing standardized data formats, communication protocols, and exchange interfaces allows disparate systems to converse freely and accurately—a digital Esperanto that unifies platforms while respecting diversity.

- **System Compatibility**

  Legacy systems often present hurdles to integration efforts. Embracing modern technologies mandates updates and adaptations, ensuring synchrony across different generations and vendors. Middleware solutions may act as intermediaries, bridging gaps and enhancing compatibility—a diplomatic mission for harmony across epochs.

- **Security and Privacy Concerns**

  As interconnectivity spreads, so too does the vulnerability to unauthorized access. Safeguarding data privacy and system integrity requires robust encryption protocols, access management, and real-time threat monitoring—ensuring that the benefits of interconnectivity do not succumb to potential exploits.

Future Horizons: A Tapestry of Connection

Envisioning the future, we foresee a tapestry where increased interconnectivity and interoperability herald limitless possibilities. Emerging technologies, like 5G, promise even quicker data exchanges, supporting complex digital twin environments with unprecedented bandwidth and speed.

Quantum computing and distributed ledger technologies offer novel avenues to enhance interconnectivity further, strengthening data synchronization and secure exchanges across the digital cosmos.

Increased interconnectivity and interoperability are not mere technical feats—they are ideological shifts toward a collaborative future where systems surface not as isolated gears, but harmonious participants within a vast, intelligent network.

As this narrative unfolds, the potential of digital twins is transformed, embodying a panorama of integrated collaboration that echoes the complexity and harmony of the natural world. It is a vision that inspires, guiding industries toward holistic solutions and innovative practices—embracing interconnectivity as a catalyst for dynamic progress and shared prosperity.

8.4 Augmented and Virtual Reality Integration

Imagine slipping on a headset and stepping into a digital domain indistinguishable from reality—a world where fantastical simulations and tangible truth converge. This is the tantalizing promise of augmented reality (AR) and virtual reality (VR), two immersive technologies that, when paired with digital twins, create powerful experiences that can transform industries and redefine how we perceive the world around us.

A Stroll Through Time: From Panoramas to Pixels

The allure of AR and VR is deeply rooted in humanity's timeless desire to transcend the boundaries of perception. In the 19th century, panoramas captivated audiences with lifelike scenes painted in 360 degrees, offering an expansive, albeit static, glimpse of faraway lands. The 20th century saw the advent of stereoscopic viewers and 3D films, modestly deepening the illusion of depth and interaction.

Fast forward, and we find ourselves entrenched in a digital renaissance, with AR and VR technology bringing to life experiences that stretch the limits of reality. The quest to merge the real with the imaginary has evolved from painted canvases to dynamic simulations, catalyzed by digital twins now capable of projecting interactive, responsive environments.

Intertwining Realities: AR and VR in Harmony with Digital Twins

Digital twins, virtual avatars of physical entities, provide fertile soil from which AR and VR flourish. Through nuanced integration, they afford users hands-on experience across domains, whether it's overlaying digital content onto real-world settings or immersing oneself in entirely fabricated realms.

Augmented Reality: Enriching the World We See

AR enhances our perception of reality by superimposing digital information onto the physical world. It elevates digital twins by providing layer upon layer of context—uniting virtual data with lived experience. With AR interfaces, digital twins spring to life in real-time, offering users the ability to visualize complex data interactively.

Consider the bustling industry of manufacturing. Here, AR can project assembly instructions directly over a product, guiding workers with precision amid intricate procedures.   The seamless blend of instructional overlays with hands-on tasks enhances efficiency, reduces errors, and bolsters employee confidence—a modern-day melding of master and apprentice guided by digital wisdom.

Similarly, engineers using AR headsets can visually inspect digital twins of building infrastructure, overlaid with real-time diagnostics and predictive maintenance cues. This augments their understanding of structural integrity, enabling faster decision-making and proactive interventions.

Virtual Reality: Crafting Immersive Experiences

VR introduces users to entirely constructed environments, offering a playground of possibilities best explored through digital twins. It plunges users into simulations that mirror real-world systems or daringly reimagine them, enhancing experiential learning and decision-making.

Within the realm of education, VR and digital twins join forces to create virtual laboratories, where students conduct experiments in physics, chemistry, or biology without the constraints of physical resources or safety concerns. This translates textbook theories into tangible exploration, animating learning with interactive, immersive visuals that deepen comprehension.

The automotive sector, too, embarks on virtual voyages. Designers and engineers venture into VR spaces to peruse digital prototypes, adjusting aesthetics or aerodynamics before physical production ensues. By simulating test drives and crash scenarios, VR enriches design considerations, ensuring vehicles meet both safety standards and aesthetic aspirations.

Applications Abound: Sectoral Successes

Embedding AR and VR with digital twins results in profound impacts across a myriad of sectors, each gaining unique vantage points from which to evolve and excel.

- **Healthcare**: Surgeons employ VR to simulate procedures, practicing complex surgeries within immersive digital realms that mirror operative environments. This enables refined skills and improved precision, ultimately enhancing patient outcomes. Meanwhile, AR applications assist with real-time surgery guidance, projecting critical data onto patient anatomies during operations.

- **Real Estate**: Potential homebuyers tour listings with VR headsets, stepping into digital twins of properties within minutes. These immersive viewings dispel geographical constraints, crafting more informed purchasing decisions. Likewise, architects leverage VR to present clients with visualizations of conceptual designs, inviting them to traverse unbuilt spaces long before they occupy reality.

- **Entertainment**: The gaming industry, a perennial pioneer of immersive experiences, harnesses VR to elevate narratives with digital twin models of character interactions, environments, and physics simulations. Game designers invite players to engage with virtual realms that respond dynamically to actions and choices, creating participatory experiences limited only by imagination's horizon.

Navigating the Challenge Course: Pathways to Integration

Though promising, the full potential of integrating AR and VR with digital twins encounters challenges that beckon for resolution.

- **Technological Limitations**:   Current AR and VR devices often grapple with limitations such as resolution fidelity, latency, and extended user discomfort.   Advancements in hardware, coupled with algorithmic efficiency, aim to enhance experience quality and reduce latency, reinvigorating widespread user adoption.

- **Data Management**: Extending the digital twin narrative into AR and VR requires robust data management capacities to process vast datasets efficiently.   Real-time synchronization across diverse devices must remain seamless, preventing interruptions while maintaining coherency in dynamic environments.

- **Interoperability**: Establishing standard protocols and interfaces is crucial for cross-platform compatibility, ensuring digital twins retain functionality regardless of the AR or VR environments they inhabit. Interoperability across different systems elucidates barriers, transforming standalone silos into interconnected virtual highways.

The Ethical Dimension: Ensuring Responsible Evolution

With great immersive power comes the responsibility to wield AR and VR ethically. Addressing concerns over virtual environments—ranging from content sensitivity to data privacy—demands ethical frameworks that balance creativity with conscientiousness.

Moreover, stakeholders must recognize the potential social implications of immersive technologies. Vigilance is required to prevent societal inequities from manifesting within AR and VR spaces, fostering inclusive practices that benefit diverse groups equitably.

As technological advancements continue to augment AR and VR capacities, digital twins promise to redefine our interaction with them. Future iterations may harness haptic feedback and neural interfaces, further blurring boundaries between human perception and digital manifestation.

These technologies will undoubtedly forge new paths, particularly when applied to achieving remote collaboration, disaster training simulations, or immersive social networking experiences. Catalyzed by innovations that enhance interactivity and realism, the fusion of AR, VR, and digital twins stands poised to unlock the boundless inclinations of an interconnected world.

The integration of AR and VR with digital twins births an unparalleled synergy that enriches perception, interaction, and innovation. These immersive technologies, united under the umbrella of digital twins, inspire industries to leap boldly towards new frontiers—crafting experiences that engage, enlighten, and empower.

In embracing this digital ballet, we journey towards spaces where digital and physical realms perform a choreographed dance of comprehension and creativity— a timeless narrative where perennial boundaries dissolve to reveal worlds anew, resonating with fascination and wonder. This transformation, layered with potential and guided by insight, invites us to traverse its landscape—eyewitnesses to the dazzling intersection of reality and imagination.

8.5 Sustainability and Environmental Impact

In an age where the clarion call of sustainability grows louder with each passing year, technology stands as both challenge and champion. Among the vanguard of innovations charging towards a more sustainable future, digital twins offer a comprehensive toolkit for understanding, modeling, and mitigating our environmental impact. With their capacity to mirror reality, run simulations, and optimize operations, digital twins become pivotal players in crafting practices that embrace our planet's health.

Historical Context: The Rise of Environmental Awareness

Revolutions in industry and technology have not come without their downsides, as mirrored by the adverse effects on the planet's ecosystems. The rapid industrialization of the 19th and 20th centuries brought unprecedented economic growth but also marked the rise of industrial pollution and resource depletion. As smoke-blackened skies and toxic waterways became common, public awareness around environmental preservation grew.

The 1960s ushered in a wave of environmental activism, leading to foundational legal measures and the birth of organizations focused on ecological preservation. Fast forward to today, and sustainability has become central to global discourse, underpinned by a collective recognition that our technological pursuits must harmonize with environmental stewardship.

Digital Twins: The Architects of Sustainability

Digital twins, the precise digital replicas of physical entities or systems, provide a sophisticated platform to simulate, analyze, and optimize processes with sustainability
in mind. Their capacity to model complexities enables
stakeholders to evaluate the environmental impact of different strategies and interventions before real-world implementation.

Efficient Resource Management

In sectors like agriculture and manufacturing, digital
twins offer granular insights into resource usage,
enabling more sustainable practices. By simulating
scenarios around water usage, energy consumption,
and raw material sourcing, digital twins inform
strategies that promote conservation and efficiency.

Consider agriculture, where precision farming revolutionizes crop production. Digital twins model fields, integrating data on soil health, weather patterns, and crop
needs. This allows farmers to optimize irrigation plans,
calibrate fertilization, and more precisely control pesti-
cide application, reducing waste and resource depletion.

Manufacturers apply digital twins to assess production
lines and supply chains, identifying opportunities to cut
energy usage and minimize waste. Factories can simulate the impact of energy-efficient technologies or sustainable materials, enabling transitions to greener operations with confidence and knowledge.

Optimizing Energy Systems

The energy sector, a nexus between technological advancement and ecological impact, finds transformative
potential in digital twins to optimize performance
and sustainability. By simulating grid operations and
integrating renewable energy sources, digital twins

fine-tune energy distribution, reducing reliance on carbon-heavy power plants and maximizing clean energy efficacy.

Utilities deploy digital twins to model demand-forecasting and grid-balancing strategies, dynamically shifting loads and harnessing renewable surpluses. This responsiveness helps to stabilize supply, reduce emissions, and support the integration of distributed energy resources, such as rooftop solar arrays or electric vehicle charging stations.

Additionally, power generation facilities use digital twins to fine-tune operations, predict equipment failures, and schedule maintenance attempts to improve efficiency and prolong asset lifetimes, ensuring that plants run greener for longer.

Urban Planning and Development

In urban planning, digital twins stand as architects of smart cities, where sustainable development and resource conservation are primary goals. By simulating traffic patterns, building usage, and infrastructure demands, city planners can develop strategies that optimize land use, transportation networks, and public services, aligning urban growth with sustainability.

Cities like Singapore utilize digital twins to monitor energy usage, traffic congestion, and public transportation efficiency. By continuously analyzing these data streams, planners can devise infrastructure changes that lower emissions, improve public transport, and create greener, more livable urban environments.

Additionally, real estate developers employ digital twins to model and reduce the environmental impact of construction projects, from energy consumption to material sourcing. They enable the sustainable design of buildings that maximize natural light and ventilation, minimizing reliance on artificial lighting and air conditioning.

Facilitating Climate Action

The pressing issue of climate change demands rapid intervention and innovative solutions. Digital twins provide valuable tools for climate scientists and policymakers to explore various climate action strategies, from carbon capture projects to reforestation initiatives.

By modeling interactions between different components of Earth's ecosystems, digital twins enable comprehensive assessment and adaptation strategies, emphasizing resilience and climate mitigation efforts. They empower decision-makers with the foresight to choose interventions that provide tangible benefits at local and global scales.

Digital twins play roles in simulating climate impact assessments of major infrastructure projects, ensuring that emissions, habitat disruption, or ecological consequences are minimized in planning stages.

Challenges and Responsible Implementation

While the promise of digital twins in sustainability is expansive, challenges persist, warranting careful implementation and consideration.

- **Data Quality and Accessibility**: Effective environmental modeling requires robust and accurate data capture from diverse sources. Ensuring data integrity and access across platforms is crucial for achieving reliable simulations, calling for continued development of interoperable data standards and integrated ecosystems.

- **Ethical Considerations**: As digital twins become

enmeshed in decision-making processes, ensuring
ethical and equitable practices remains vital. Models must be developed and interpreted with transparency, avoiding biases that could adversely affect disadvantaged communities or ecological systems.

- **Energy Use**: The computational power required
  for comprehensive digital twin models raises questions about their energy consumption. Balancing
  the energy use of modeling with the sustainability
  strategies they promote is an ongoing concern that
  calls for innovations in energy-efficient computing.

The Path Forward: Towards a Sustainable Tomorrow

The path to sustainable development is one of
innovation, cooperation, and accountability. As digital
twins become more sophisticated and widespread,
their contributions to sustainability must be optimized
through cross-industry collaboration, regulatory
frameworks, and public engagement.

Harnessing digital twins entails not only developing the
technology but cultivating a global commitment to sustainable practices that leverage it as a key driver of posi-
tive environmental change.

In the emerging narrative where digital twins
collaborate with sustainability, a synergistic symphony
emerges. This harmonious concert between technology
and ecology offers the precision needed to protect and
enhance our world.

By optimizing energy systems, enhancing resource management, guiding urban development, and informing climate action, digital twins carve pathways toward a resilient future where innovation aligns with the planet's
needs.

In this pursuit, let us become steadfast caretakers of the earth, using digital twins as instruments to orchestrate sustainable harmony—where technology serves as a compassionate steward and architect of renewed environmental abundance.

Chapter 9

Ethical Considerations and Privacy in Digital Twin Use

Ethical considerations and privacy concerns are pivotal in digital twin deployment, particularly regarding data collection and usage. Ensuring data privacy safeguards and addressing ownership and control disputes are crucial to maintaining trust. The ethical use of simulations in decision-making processes must also be scrutinized. Navigating complex regulatory and compliance landscapes poses additional challenges. This chapter delves into these ethical and privacy issues, highlighting their significance in responsible digital twin implementation and the development of frameworks to ensure accountability and public trust.

9.1   Data Privacy Concerns

In the digital twins' gala of innovation, where virtual counterparts reflect and predict the behavior of their physical siblings, the relentless rhythm of data collection beats at its heart. This ocean of data, rich with potential, is nevertheless fraught with perils concerning

individual privacy and ethical stewardship. As our
world increasingly wraps itself in the warm embrace
of connectivity, the notion of data privacy takes center
stage, demanding vigilance and responsibility in equal
measure.

A Historical Prelude: Privacy in the Age of Information

The journey to our current moment began in a pre-
digital past where privacy meant opaque curtains and
whispered conversations. With the advent of the digital
revolution, the rules of the game changed irreversibly.
Information that was once confined to ink and paper
transformed into endless streams of ones and zeros,
crisscrossing the globe at the speed of light.

In the 1960s and 70s, the rise of computer databases
raised early alarms about data privacy—a harbinger
of today's debates. Fears about the state's surveillance
capabilities echoed through public discourse, exemplified by George Orwell's dystopian imaginings. As the
internet era dawned, data privacy evolved into a daily
concern transcending borders and impacting every
industry.

The Double-Edged Sword of Data Collection

Digital twins leverage diverse datasets to create holistic, dynamic models that enhance predictability and efficiency. Yet, these datasets often encompass sensitive
and personal information, transforming the digital twin
from a mere technological marvel to a vigilant guardian
of privacy rights.

Imagine a healthcare setting, where digital twins
harness medical records to optimize treatment paths.
These records, including intimate patient details,
are indispensable for effective modeling.   Yet, in

an interconnected digital cosmos, such data can inadvertently become vulnerable to breaches or unauthorized access—a delicate balance of power requiring steadfast governance.

Potential Risks: Navigating the Privacy Landscape

- **Data Breaches and Unauthorized Access**: The transition to digitalization amplifies the danger of unauthorized access and data breaches. In the hands of malicious actors, compromised personal data can lead to a wide array of consequences, from identity theft to reputational damage. Digital twins, dependent on vast quantities of data, must implement fortresses of security to shield sensitive information from malevolent intentions.

- **Surveillance and Profiling Risks**: The perpetual flow of data in digital twin systems raises valid concerns of surveillance. There lies the uncomfortable possibility of constant monitoring, where data is harvested not solely for innovations but for capturing personal behavior and tendencies. This not only fuels profiling fears but also instills apprehension over the potential for discrimination and bias.

- **Data Ownership and Consent**: The question of who owns the aggregated data is equally significant. Without clear ownership demarcations, conflicts arise between individuals, corporations, and governments. It is vital to ensure that individuals retain agency over their data, permitting usage only when conferred with informed consent and transparency.

Case Studies: Real-World Insights

205

- **The Healthcare Conundrum**: In hospitals, digital twins revolutionize patient care pathways, individualizing treatment approaches. However, issues arise concerning informed consent: Do patients fully comprehend how their data is used, and do they have control over its application and lifespan?

- **Smart City Initiatives**: Cities embracing comprehensive digital infrastructure face scrutiny over procedural transparency. As public spaces become smart, widespread data collection risks turning surveillance into reality. For example, urban traffic flow optimization through digital twins might inadvertently result in continuous vehicle tracking.

- **Commercial Applications**: Consider retail giants that deploy digital twins to analyze consumer preferences and optimize shopping experiences. While such data enhances sales strategies, it raises ethical questions about consumer consent and the permanence of collected data profiles.

Proactive Measures: Preserving Privacy

Ensuring data privacy demands a concerted effort across technological, legislative, and cultural domains.

- **Robust Data Encryption**: Encrypting data both at rest and in transit is a non-negotiable safeguard, ensuring that sensitive information remains indecipherable to unauthorized entities.

- **Data Anonymization and Minimization**: Anonymizing datasets can protect privacy by stripping identifying information while maintaining analytics' utility. Moreover, adhering to data minimization principles—collecting only what is absolutely necessary—reduces exposure risk.

- **Transparency and Accountability**: Lifecycles of data within digital twins require transparency. Clearly communicated privacy policies and data practices build stakeholder trust, fostering a culture of openness reliant on accountability.

Regulatory Frameworks: Global Perspectives

Navigating data privacy involves adhering to evolving national and regional regulations that aim to reconcile advancement with respect for individual rights. Landmark legislative acts such as the European Union's General Data Protection Regulation (GDPR) underscore the importance of privacy as a fundamental human right.

These regulations enforce strict guidelines for data collection, usage, and storage. Digital twin practitioners are required to comply with data protection laws, embedding privacy into the very architecture of these systems—a necessary covenant with society.

Future Outlook: A Balancing Act of Innovation and Ethics

As digital twin technologies advance, the focus on privacy must continue to evolve. Emerging technologies, such as homomorphic encryption and blockchain, promise innovative methods for securing data without compromising its utility.

Building an ethical framework for responsible innovation means incorporating privacy-by-design methodologies—approaching data systems with privacy considerations integrated from their inception.

It promotes a collaborative environment where technology serves people powerfully yet respectfully.

The discourse on data privacy within the realm of digital twins is a narrative interwoven with challenge and opportunity. The balance must be delicately maintained between technological marvels and the sanctity of individual rights, ensuring that data-driven innovation serves humanity without overstepping ethical boundaries.

Stakeholders in digital twin deployment must embody a dual role as innovators and guardians, crafting a future where trust and privacy echo through every heartbeat of this digital evolution. As we push the frontiers of what technology can achieve, let us remain vigilant custodians, honoring the private sanctuaries of personal data and cultivating an ethical legacy worthy of inheritance. A future where innovation thrives amidst respect—a symphony where technology harmonizes with humanity's values.

9.2   Ethical Implications of Simulation

In the world of digital twins, where virtual realms mirror the intricacies of reality with staggering precision, we find ourselves standing at the crossroads of philosophical quandaries and technological wonders. As simulations become critical components in decision-making, wielding influence over vast landscapes—from urban planning to healthcare—the ethical implications they harbor demand rigorous inspection. The question looms large: As we construct ever more sophisticated simulations, how do we ensure that these virtual dynamics translate ethically into the real world?

Tracing the Roots: A Historical Retrospective

Historically, the concept of simulation has captivated human imagination. The earliest forms of simulation can be seen in tactical military exercises and strategic games, employed by ancient civilizations to mimic war scenarios and devise strategies. With the dawn of the computer age, simulations adopted a digital veneer, rapidly advancing in complexity and application as processing power burgeoned.

By the 20th century, simulations found homes in scientific and engineering spheres, enabling the virtual testing of theories, designs, and products before physical production ensued. From aircraft aerodynamics to molecular structures, virtual experimentation provided a cost-effective and safe environment for refinement and exploration.

As simulation technology intertwined with digital twins, a new dimension emerged—one where simulations impact real-world outcomes and hold ethical implications in their virtual grasp.

Simulation in Decision Making: Virtue or Vice?

The allure of simulations lies in their promise to distill complexity into manageable insights, allowing stakeholders to explore potential futures and make informed decisions. Yet this power contemplates ethical dimensions akin to uncharted waters—where the risks and responsibilities multiply.

- **Bias in Simulations**
  Simulations are the products of their creators, which means that inherent biases can subtly seep into underlying algorithms, skewing outcomes. In an urban planning simulation evaluating residential zoning, for example, biased data may inadvertently reinforce socio-economic disparities, prompting decisions that disadvantage certain

209

communities.

Preventing such bias necessitates vigilance—ensuring a diverse dataset, encompassing varied perspectives, and employing transparent algorithms. Ethical oversight throughout simulation development mandates critical assessment and continuous auditing to ensure outcomes honor equity and fairness.

- **The Illusion of Accuracy**
  While simulations promise predictive power, their accuracy hinges on underlying assumptions and data quality. Overreliance on simulations can cultivate an illusion of certainty, potentially leading decision-makers astray if they neglect the broader context of uncertainty inherent in any model.

  Take financial markets, where risk assessment simulations guide trading strategies. A simulation based on incomplete data or erroneous assumptions can amplify economic risks rather than mitigate them. Users must pair the seductive allure of simulation with prudent skepticism and contextual understanding, employing simulations as guides rather than fortunetellers.

- **Ethical Responsibility in High-Stakes Domains**
  In high-stakes environments—such as healthcare and environmental policy—simulation-informed decisions can have profound repercussions. Digital twins simulating patient responses to treatment protocols or strategies for climate intervention wield significant influence over lives and ecological futures.

  With this power comes an ethical responsibility to uphold the highest standards of precision and care. Simulations must be rigorously validated and peer-reviewed, and decision-makers should maintain an awareness of the moral weight their choices entail—grounded in respect for human and environmental dignity.

Applications Illuminating Ethical Dimensions

- **Healthcare Simulations**
  On the frontier of medical innovation, simulations facilitate the virtual testing of treatment strategies, reducing risks associated with trial-and-error methods. They personalize medicine by simulating individual patient outcomes—enhancing the likelihood of success and minimizing adverse effects. However, ethical considerations demand meticulous attention to data integrity and patient consent, ensuring simulations support informed, equitable care.

- **Autonomous Vehicles**
  In the race toward autonomy, vehicle simulations serve as proving grounds, testing navigation systems, safety features, and decision-making algorithms. Yet, ethical challenges surface around AI accountability and liability in unforeseen scenarios. Ensuring designs reflect ethical principles involves balancing safety, transparency, and trust within developmental frameworks.

- **Disaster Management**
  Disaster response strategies benefit from simulation models predicting diverse scenarios—natural or manmade. Cities simulate evacuation procedures, resource allocations, and emergency protocols. Ethical implementation requires prioritizing actions is safeguarding vulnerable

populations and ensuring no community is
marginalized in strategic planning.

Ethical Frameworks: Balancing Virtue and Innovation

Embracing ethical considerations in simulation design
and implementation requires a multi-faceted approach:

- **Inclusive Collaboration**
  Engaging stakeholders, including ethicists,
  community representatives, and policymakers,
  creates a symphony of perspectives that fosters
  ethical integrity. Incorporating feedback
  throughout simulation development enhances
  relevance and societal value.

- **Transparency and Explainability**
  Adopting the principles of transparency in simulation logic and decision pathways is crucial. Clear,
  understandable documentation of model assumptions and decisions allows stakeholders to evaluate the simulations' scope and limitations, building
  trust and accountability.

- **Continuous Education and Training**
  Equipping innovators and practitioners with
  ethical literacy promotes a culture of responsibility. Programs focusing on ethical reasoning,
  data ethics, and bias identification empower
  professionals to recognize and mitigate ethical
  dilemmas in practice.

Navigating the Future: Ethical Stewardship in the Dig-
ital Age

As digital twins and simulations continue to advance,
ethical stewardship must remain at the forefront of tech-

nological innovation. Organizations must proactively establish ethical frameworks that align with societal values, recognizing that the trust placed in simulations is both a responsibility and a privilege.

Emerging technologies, such as quantum computing and neural networks, promise even greater simulation capabilities, amplifying both potential and responsibility. Vigilance, foresight, and ethical collaboration illuminate the path ahead, ensuring that simulations enrich human experiences and contribute to a just, equitable world.

It is through harnessing the collective intelligence that we can tackle humanity's most pressing challenges, pushing the boundaries of potential to forge a brighter, innovative future. As individuals and organizations embrace the symphony of collaboration, they not only enhance their own prospects but contribute to the greater tapestry of human progress.

9.3 Ownership and Control of Data

In a world where digital footprints expand with each passing moment, the concepts of data ownership and control emerge as both cornerstone and conundrum. Like ancient artisans crafting timeless scrolls, today's technologists collect and harness data—a resource both elusive and indispensable. Yet, who truly holds the reins to this digital realm? Beneath the surface of digital twin technology, questions of ownership and control ripple outwards, challenging conventions and igniting debates that stretch from boardrooms to legislatures.

A Historical Perspective: From Tangible Property to Intangible Assets

In bygone eras, property was a tangible affair—land,

gold, and livestock defined wealth and power. The Industrial Revolution marked the era where knowledge began to balance the scales alongside physical assets. As industries evolved, so too did concepts of ownership, with patents and intellectual property safeguarding innovation.

Fast forward to the digital age. Data, unlike traditional assets, defies easy categorization. It is simultaneously abundant and precise, residing in clouds rather than vaults. And with this evolution, the questions of who owns and controls data—personal or organizational—have become pervasive and complex.

Who Owns the Data? Navigating the New Frontier

At the heart of digital twin technology, data flows from countless sources: machines on the factory floor, sensors in smart cities, human inputs in healthcare systems. But as this data converges, the question remains: Who are the rightful custodians, and what claims can individuals and entities lay upon it?

- **Individuals as Data Generators**: In many instances, individuals produce the data—consider wearable health devices, smart thermostats, or even social media activity. While individuals generate data, they often relinquish aspects of control as technologies aggregate and analyze it. The balance between empowerment and transparency becomes pivotal, ensuring individuals possess a clear understanding of how their data is utilized.

- **Corporate Custodians**: Organizations argue that their role as data processors grants them ownership over curated datasets. In industries where value is derived from analytics—be it predictive maintenance in manufacturing or consumer insights in retail—companies assert control over data as a critical asset. However, it's essential they recognize their custodial role, maintaining ethical stewardship and lawful boundaries.

- **The Public Domain**: When data pertains to societal infrastructure or environmental health, questions arise about its communal ownership. Should insights from smart grid data serve collective public interest, perhaps guiding policy for sustainable development? Finding a balance between private interests and the public good demands strategies that advance society while respecting individual and corporate rights.

Establishing Control: The Pillars of Governance

The orchestration of control hinges on implementing robust frameworks that delineate rights, responsibilities, and remedies across stakeholders. Effective governance ensures equitable management while mitigating risks associated with data commoditization and exploitation.

- **Policy and Regulation**: Regulatory bodies maintain oversight through frameworks that enshrine data protection and establish clear ownership rights. Legislations like the European Union's General Data Protection Regulation (GDPR) provide individuals with clarity and control over their data, ensuring entities operate transparently and respectfully within statutory bounds.

- **Consent and Transparency**: Transparent practices that seek informed consent serve as foundational

pillars for ethical ownership and control. By
empowering individuals with choice and
information, organizations foster trust and
cultivate relationships grounded in integrity and
accountability.

- **Data Contracts and Agreements**: Formal
agreements can outline data sharing arrangements
and ownership terms between entities. Contracts
specify conditions, usage rights, and termination
clauses, protecting stakeholders and facilitating
lawful collaboration.

Practical Applications and Case Studies

- **Healthcare**: Consider healthcare networks where
digital twins simulate treatment journeys based on
patient data. While such simulations drive precision medicine, tensions arise around who owns the
collected digital health insights. Balancing innovation with patient autonomy calls for nuanced policies that prioritize ethical data usage.

- **Smart Cities**: In smart cities, data from
interconnected systems informs urban planning,
traffic management, and public services. While
municipal bodies champion efficiency and
development, citizens' rights over their data
footprint must remain paramount. City planners
are urged to implement transparent policies,
inviting public dialogue and ensuring an equitable
exchange.

- **Financial Services**: Within finance, digital twins
enable real-time assessments of market conditions
and risk factors. Institutions argue for ownership

of processed insights leveraged for competitive advantage, yet they are bound to respect privacy obligations and regulatory frameworks—aligning innovation with responsibility.

Emerging Models and Future Considerations

As technology advances, new ownership frameworks emerge, challenging existing paradigms. Consider decentralized data models such as those enabled by blockchain technology. By decentralizing control, data ownership becomes distributed, engaging broader stakeholders and enhancing trust through transparency and immutability.

These evolving models prompt exploration into data cooperatives, where members collectively own and monetarily benefit from shared datasets. Such initiatives foster community-based decision-making and address inequalities within data economies—a testament to collaborative potential in redefining ownership and agency.

The Ethical Horizon: Balancing Rights and Returns

Data ownership is a narrative with ethical undertones, requiring a commitment to balance interests amid dynamic landscapes. Organizations should strive to relinquish exploitative practices, ensuring technology amplifies human potential while safeguarding rights. Emphasizing fairness, equity, and respect within data strategies becomes crucial for shaping a digitally-inclusive future.

Stakeholders across sectors are called to engage dialogue that reconciles profitability with accountability, mitigating potential power imbalances and driving responsible innovation—advocating technologies that serve people rather than subjugating them.

It is through harnessing the collective intelligence that

we can tackle humanity's most pressing challenges, pushing the boundaries of potential to forge a brighter, innovative future. As individuals and organizations embrace the symphony of collaboration, they not only enhance their own prospects but contribute to the greater tapestry of human progress.

Emerging as guardians rather than gatekeepers, we build a legacy where technology and humanity thrive cohesively, inspiring confidence, compassion, and co-creation in the digital era. Let us endeavor toward a vision where ownership clarifies rather than complicates, anchoring human dignity within the dynamic expanse of technological evolution.

9.4 Regulatory and Compliance Challenges

As digital twin technology surges forth, crafting a brave new world where virtual twins mirror and manage every facet of the physical realm, the regulatory landscape must adapt with grace and vigilance. No longer can regulators afford to merely tiptoe around technological advances; instead, they must embrace their roles as stewards ensuring that innovation progresses within ethical and legal frameworks. Navigating this terrain is anything but straightforward, with challenges abundant and solutions elusive.

A Historical Glimpse: From Industrial to Digital Regulation

Since the dawn of industry, regulation has been the scaffold around which societal progress is built, ensuring that technological leaps do not come at the expense of public welfare. Whether it was the introduction of railway standards in the 19th century or the environmental regulations of the 20th, the dance between innovation and regulation has been an ongoing saga of tension and resolution.

As the digital age unfurls, ushering in a tapestry woven with data and connectivity, regulatory frameworks must now interface with ephemeral bits and bytes as much as bricks and mortar. The challenge lies in crafting policies that are both resilient to change and wise enough to anticipate future needs.

Navigating the Seas of Data Privacy and Security

One of the preeminent challenges in regulating digital twins arises from data privacy concerns. With digital twins relying on a constant influx of data from myriad sources, the potential for misuse or breach is significant. Regulatory bodies are tasked with safeguarding personal information and ensuring that data is only used with consent, in a manner that respects individual rights.

The General Data Protection Regulation (GDPR) of the European Union exemplifies a comprehensive approach to privacy, mandating transparency and accountability from organizations handling personal data. However, the global nature of digital data presents challenges of jurisdiction and enforcement, as regulations vary across borders.

Maintaining Ethical Standards in Simulation and AI

As digital twins often employ advanced simulations and AI, ensuring these tools are used ethically remains paramount. Algorithms that underpin simulations may inadvertently perpetuate biases if not carefully monitored and calibrated. This potential for unintended bias demands regulatory scrutiny to ensure fairness and equity.

For example, consider digital twins used in urban planning, where simulations inform decisions about zoning and infrastructure. Inequitable algorithms could inadvertently marginalize vulnerable communities if unchecked. Regulators play a critical role in establishing standards that uphold ethical considerations, ensuring that simulations serve as tools of inclusivity rather than division.

Challenges of Interoperability and Standardization

The beauty of digital twins lies in their interconnectedness, but this also poses a significant regulatory challenge. Achieving interoperability—where digital twins seamlessly exchange data across platforms and industries—requires standardized protocols and open data formats. Regulators must strike a balance between encouraging innovation and minimizing friction between disparate systems.

This challenge is particularly evident in industries like healthcare, where digital twins simulate patient care pathways. Ensuring interoperability between electronic health records, monitoring devices, and treatment algorithms necessitates coordination between manufacturers, healthcare providers, and regulators to establish common standards.

Case Studies: Regulatory Challenges in Action

- 1. **Autonomous Vehicles:** As self-driving technology advances, digital twins simulate vehicular behavior under myriad conditions to ensure safety. However, regulatory frameworks governing liability and responsibility lag behind technological progress. Policymakers must navigate questions about accountability—who is responsible in the event of an accident, the manufacturer of the autonomous vehicle, its operator, or the digital twin developer?

- **2. Environmental Applications:** Digital twins model ecosystems to guide conservation efforts and monitor natural resources. While these insights are valuable, regulatory challenges arise concerning data collection, sovereignty, and indigenous rights. Crafting policies that protect ecosystems while respecting local communities requires a nuanced, culturally sensitive approach.

Balancing Innovation with Regulation

Striking the right balance between fostering innovation and instituting regulation is an ongoing, dynamic process. Regulators must remain agile, adapting to technological advances without stifling creativity or competitiveness.

- **1. Proactive Regulatory Design:** Regulations should adopt a forward-looking approach, anticipating technological trajectories and establishing flexible frameworks that accommodate evolving scenarios. Proactive engagement with industry stakeholders allows for collaborative regulation, where insights from innovators inform policy design.

- **2. Multi-Stakeholder Collaboration:** Effective regulation often benefits from the collective wisdom of policymakers, industry leaders, academics, and civil society. This collaboration enhances regulatory legitimacy and fosters environments where digital twin technology can thrive while minimizing adverse impacts.

- **3. Encouraging Best Practices:** Regulatory agencies can promote best practices by recognizing and rewarding organizations that demonstrate leadership in ethical data management, security, and sustainability. Economic incentives and public recognition play pivotal roles in encouraging industry standards of excellence.

The Path Ahead: Regulatory Innovation and Evolution

As digital twins continue to reshape industry landscapes, regulatory innovation becomes essential. Emerging technologies such as blockchain offer innovative pathways for secure data management and transparent auditing, supporting regulatory objectives.

Regulators may also consider sandbox approaches, where novel applications of digital twins receive temporary exemptions from certain regulations to encourage experimentation. This iterative learning fosters regulatory innovation alongside technological progression.

Regulating digital twin technology amidst a whirlwind of rapid technological advances is no small feat. It necessitates a delicate interplay between guidance and restraint, fostering environments where creativity and responsibility coexist harmoniously.

Through informed, adaptive, and collaborative approaches, regulators can ensure that digital twins are harnessed as powerful tools for progress, optimizing their potential while safeguarding public interests. As shepherds of the digital frontier, regulators hold a crucial role in shaping a future where technology enhances human welfare, serving as stewards of an ethical, equitable, and enlightened digital society.

9.5 Building Trust in Digital Twin Systems

In the era of digital transformation, trust is the golden thread weaving through the technological narrative, linking the nodes of innovation to the fabric of human experience. As digital twin systems ascend in importance, becoming the virtual proxy of our reality, establishing and maintaining trust in these systems becomes paramount. This journey is both art and science, ensconcing technical robustness with the softer, equally nuanced elements of transparency, reliability, and ethics.

A Stroll Through Time: Trust and Technology

The dance between trust and technology is as ancient as the invention of the wheel. Each technological leap—from the printing press to the steam engine—has come tethered to skepticism. Yet, over time, as communities understood and observed consistent reliability and benefits, trust naturally followed.

Consider the early days of electricity, when flickers from newly installed bulbs were met with wary eyes. Yet through reliability, governed by safety standards and transparency, electricity entrenched itself as indispensable. Likewise, digital twin systems must traverse this continuum of trust-building, from skepticism to acceptance.

Trust: The Nexus of Transparency and Reliability

Digital twins, as comprehensive simulators of reality, must exude transparency. But what does this mean in practice? It entails clear communication about how digital twins collect and process data, make predictions, and ensure privacy. Users need assurance that these digital counterparts reflect the most accurate and

223

unbiased representation of reality.

- **Transparency and Openness**

  A cornerstone of trust is transparency. Providing clear insight into how digital twins operate, including algorithms and data sources, fosters confidence. This transparency can be framed through accessible documentation and user-friendly interfaces translating the inner workings of the system for a wider audience.

  For instance, a city deploying digital twins for urban planning may involve citizens by sharing insights and predictions on public forums. By doing so, residents gain assurance about the rationale behind infrastructure decisions, thereby fostering communal trust and shared agendas.

- **Reliability and Consistency**

  A digital twin's credibility hinges on its consistency—providing reliable predictions even amidst evolving data. This demands rigorous testing and validation, ensuring digital twins withstand changing conditions. Organizations must demonstrate these systems' performance over time, much like a musician hitting the right note on every occasion to gain an audience's trust.

  Examples abound in aerospace, where digital twins model aircraft engine components. Engine manufacturers like Rolls-Royce test systems extensively, guaranteeing accuracy and reliability of performance predictions—a critical factor when human lives hang in the balance.

Establishing Ethical Foundations

Trust also dances on the ethics stage. Upholding ethical standards throughout digital twin deployment builds trust by ensuring the technology aligns with societal values.

- **Ethical Design and Implementation**

  Design choices must reflect ethical considerations—from preventing bias in algorithms to safeguarding personal data. Ethical frameworks guide developers and stakeholders, fostering a culture of responsibility and adherence to normative values.

  Consider healthcare systems deploying digital twins to simulate patient treatment paths. Ethical design involves equipping clinicians with holistic insights that ensure equitable care, proactively addressing potential algorithmic biases affecting minority groups.

- **Stakeholder Engagement and Dialogue**

  Engaging stakeholders—whether clients, users, or the general public—enhances trust through open dialogue and involvement. By incorporating diverse perspectives and addressing concerns upfront, digital twin developers foster inclusivity and collective ownership of outcomes.

  In environmental management, stakeholder dialogue ensures that digital twin projections align with community and ecological concerns, establishing credibility and unified action toward conservation goals.

Communication: Bridging the Digital Divide

Communicative fluency transforms technical prowess into tangible trust. Clear and open communication

ensures users comprehend how digital twins function
and appreciate the value they provide.

- **User Education and Empowerment**

  Empowering users through education builds
  awareness and capability. Training programs,
  workshops, and intuitive interfaces demystify
  digital twin technology, emphasizing its benefits
  and relevance.

  Manufacturers employing digital twins for
  predictive maintenance may host educational
  seminars, enlightening operators and technicians
  about system functionalities, methodology, and
  troubleshooting capabilities.

- **Crisis Management and Responsiveness**

  Trust is tested and often solidified during crises.
  Establishing clear protocols for crisis management
  ensures rapid, effective responses, reassuring
  stakeholders that digital twins embed resilience.

  Consider supply chain disruptions due to
  unforeseen circumstances. Swift adaptation
  by digital twins in adjusting logistics routes and
  inventory management exemplifies proactive
  crisis response, cementing stakeholder trust.

Real-Life Trust Paradigms

- **Automotive Reliability**

  Automotive manufacturers engage rigorous
  validation processes to certify the dependability
  of digital twins employed in self-driving
  technologies. By showcasing iterative testing
  cycles and incorporating public feedback, firms
  align innovation with consumer trust.

- **Financial Transparency**

  In finance, digital twin systems utilize transparent algorithms to model and predict market trends. Financial institutions achieve trust by illustrating model accuracy and sharing methodologies with stakeholders, fostering trust in digital solutions driving investment decisions.

Future Trajectories: Continual Trust Building

The journey of trust-building in digital twin systems evolves as technologies and societal expectations grow more complex. Emerging technologies like blockchain offer decentralization futures, enhancing transparency and trust through immutable transaction records.

Further, adopting AI Transparency codes ensures that autonomous digital twins provide explainable outputs, demystifying results with contextual clarifications.

Ultimately, trust in digital twin systems is not a destination reached and forgotten; it is a continuous commitment, a promise sustained through every interaction and innovation. By fostering transparency, reliability, and open communication, digital twin practitioners craft a narrative where technology serves as an unwavering ally—a trustworthy partner navigating the intricate dance of progress.

In this digital union, we must champion trust-by-design—ensuring technology enriches humanity's potential while respecting its ethos. As we journey forth, let us sculpt a future where digital twins illuminate paths defined by understanding, cooperation, and trust, breathing vibrant life into our shared digital destinies.

www.ingramcontent.com/pod-product-compliance
Lightning Source LLC
Chambersburg PA
CBHW070942050326
40689CB00014B/3311